ALLERGY INFORMATION ASSOCIATION

# The Food Allergy Cookbook

DIETS UNLIMITED FOR LIMITED DIETS

ALLERGY INFORMATION ASSOCIATION

# The Food Allergy Cookbook

## DIETS UNLIMITED FOR LIMITED DIETS

St. Martin's Press
New York

Originally published in Canada under the title *The Allergy Cookbook* by Methuen Publications.

Library of Congress Cataloging in Publication Data
Main entry under title:

The Food allergy cookbook.

Includes index.
1. Food allergy—Diet therapy—Recipes.   I. Allergy
Information Association.
RC596.F655   1984      641.5′631      84-3386
ISBN 0-312-66432-X (pbk.)

First U.S. Edition

10 9 8 7 6 5 4 3 2 1

# Contents

# Acknowledgments

It is said that the creation of a cookbook is never the work of one individual. This is especially true for this cookbook. Many people have helped in its preparation. Numerous hours were spent in the test kitchens of Kingsmill Foods evaluating, combining and creating recipes. The task of creating the original cookbook fell to Wilma Verch and then to Marg Pollard. To this nucleus were added the efforts of Thalia Considine, Lin McKenzie, and Mary Tutty, who tested, tried and suggested. A large measure of thanks is due to Rosalind Jordan for typing, secretarial services and invaluable moral support; and to Kathy Miller, Wilma Verch and Jackie Rosati for proofreading. Deep thanks to Shell Canada Ltd. and H.J. Heinz Company of Canada Ltd. for their financial contribution. A special thanks to Laurie Daglish for her inspiration in the conception of this cookbook, accepting the challenging task of researching and organizing the thousands of contributions, and for her triumphs and defeats in testing the recipes.

*To all those everywhere who were put on a diet to avoid lemons and figured out how to make lemonade.*

# Foreword

On Christmas Eve 1964, I gave my whiny 10-month-old baby a sip of my non-alcoholic eggnog. Within minutes she had turned a strange color and was experiencing great difficulty breathing. We rushed her to the hospital. The diagnosis, after many anxious hours, was "severe allergic reaction." For almost two weeks she remained in hospital for further testing and treatment, and eggs and milk were identified as but two of the many items to which she was sensitive.

We brought her home loaded with instructions for care and feeding—no eggs, no milk, no wheat; only lamb, carrots, squash, soy, rice, bananas and pears. I was lost. At the time there was no labelling on foods to guide me and the hospital had given me only two recipes which would not meet the standards for inclusion in this cookbook today.

So I set out to find other sources of information. A popular magazine advised that it contained "allergy" recipes. I eagerly bought it. What a disappointment! Recipes which were milk-free used eggs, and vice versa. Then a relative found an allergy cookbook. It did not help either, since the only substitute suggested for wheat was potato, which was also off-limits for my daughter.

Finally, after a year of struggling, someone told me about a group of mothers like myself who had begun an organization called "Allergy Information." I joined and received their cookbook and a subscription to their newsletter. *Diets Unlimited for Limited Diets* comprised 10 looseleaf pages offering about 50 recipes. At first I was disappointed. I had paid $3.00 and there was only one recipe I could use! But as the newsletters began arriving, I learned to substitute: when a recipe called for a cup of wheat flour, I could make it with $7/8$ cup of rice flour. I found three more recipes that I could use. Then I learned that if I let the rice flour mixture sit for an hour before adding the leavening and finishing the baking, the product was much tastier and more cohesive. With each little suggestion from the

7

network of members, I was able to use additional recipes, transform family favorites and utilize standard cookbooks. My daughter remained on very few foods for many years, but her meals were varied and appealing because of the help I had from Allergy Information.

For about 20 years, Allergy Information Association has provided an extensive service that helps patients live a normal, healthy life by dealing with their allergies sensibly and knowledgeably. Now the cookbook has been completely revised based on these years of experience, incorporating input from members and dietitians. There is something here for everyone, no matter how restricted the diet.

Variety in meal planning can be achieved once you become adept at managing the foods allowed on any restricted diet. With this cookbook, we hope to show you how to do just that.

SUSAN DAGLISH
Toronto, 1983

# Introduction

The intent of this cookbook is to outline a method for dealing with food allergies. The only sure method of controlling food allergy is removing the sensitizing food from the diet for a period of time. This is simple enough for strawberries or rutabaga, but requires considerable effort, ingenuity and caution if the allergic foods are milk, wheat or eggs. Removing a food from the diet, however, may be so restricting that the resulting lifestyle becomes more problematic than the symptom-filled period before the allergen was identified.

The term food allergy implies that there has been a specific response to a food leading to the development of allergic-type antibodies. When these antibodies are present, they react with the particular food ingested to produce an allergic reaction. Symptoms may be relieved in a number of ways. Antihistamines can help such symptoms as hives, swelling and nose symptoms; ingested cromoglycate can sometimes reduce the intensity and frequency of reactions in the intestines and perhaps other reactions. But again, the only sure method of control is removing the sensitizing food from the diet.

The natural history of food allergies provides some reason for hope. They most commonly appear in early childhood and frequently subside as the child grows older. However, food allergies can appear for the first time in adults. Cow's milk, wheat, eggs, corn, nuts and legumes are among the common offending foods.

Some types of food intolerance are not due to allergy. That is, there is no immune response to antibody present, and therefore, allergic-type symptoms such as swelling about the mouth, shortness of breath, hives or collapse are not present. One example is lactose intolerance. The affected individual has a deficiency of the enzyme lactase which breaks down the milk sugar, lactose. Ingestion of milk then leads to various digestive symptoms, including vomiting, excess gas, cramps and diarrhea. A preparation containing the enzyme lactase can be purchased and placed in milk to help digest the milk sugar; milk ingestion is then tolerated. Celiac disease is another example of intolerance. While much is known about the disease, the reason why it affects some people has not been yet determined. The treatment is an avoidance of the offending substance, generally for the lifetime of the person.

Symptoms can be eliminated or greatly reduced by vigilant control of environment and diet. A proper balance between unreasonable zeal and inadequate attention to health is difficult to achieve but desirable. It is evident that one cookbook cannot be expected to provide all the answers and a variety of sources should be used. Nevertheless, it is hoped that this cookbook will provide a great deal of dietary aid for the allergic member of the family.

JERRY DOLOVICH
M.D., F.R.C.P.(C)

# How To Use This Cookbook

What do you do with a recipe that looks appetizing but uses ingredients which are not acceptable to your diet, or includes refined ingredients which you may want to replace with more wholesome ones? If you have been rejecting recipes that look almost good enough to eat, this cookbook will help you learn how to tailor recipes to your own needs.

The first step is obviously finding recipes which are available to you with a minimum of tailoring. Use the index. Each recipe is listed alphabetically with the page number beside it, of course, but there is also a legend for each recipe listing allergens: M for milk, E for egg, W for wheat, G for gluten, C for corn, S for sugar and F for salicylate (Feingold). If the recipe eliminates one, it will be marked with a ‡ If it can easily be adapted to eliminate an allergen, it will be marked with an asterisk (*). A glance will tell you which recipes are suitable for your diet.

Each recipe itself is coded in the same way. In the shaded box to the left of the recipe there are three categories: Free of, could be free of and contains. "Free of" means the recipe does not call for that ingredient. "Could be free of" means the recipe is easily adapted to avoid that ingredient. For example, a recipe lists butter as an ingredient and the legend indicates "could be free of: M." By substituting milk-free margarine, the recipe becomes milk free. As another example, a recipe lists oil. The legend will indicate "could be free of: C, F," because many oils are made of corn and contain the preservative BHT which is not allowed on a Feingold diet. It is easy to use an oil which is free of both. When there is an ingredient in the "could be free of" section, it is designated beside that ingredient in the recipe — 1 cup oil (*C, F). A final example is for gluten sensitive persons. Recipes calling for oats, millet and wheat starch are designated "could be free of G" because some gluten-sensitive persons can use them.

Once you have tried the recipes that are immediately suitable, try some that list ingredients which you cannot use, and adapt them. Following are some guides for substitution. When you feel more confident, you will be able to assess new recipes and adapt them for your own use.

11

*Milk Free:* Most recipes listing milk (not condensed or specially treated milk) can use goat's milk or soy milk, or water or fruit juice with a bit more fat. When butter is called for, use milk-free margarine.

*Egg Free:* Try recipe egg free or with an Egg Replacer if eggs need not be separated. This will work about 80 percent of the time.

*Wheat Free:* We have done our best to provide recipes with various kinds of flours, so that there should be something for everyone. Refer to the section *Substitutes and Suggestions.*

*Gluten Free:* Accepted gluten sources are wheat, rye and barley. Some people find they cannot tolerate oats or millet, others find they cannot tolerate wheat starch. You should consult a medical advisor before testing your limits.

*Corn Free:* The association of corn producers proudly claim that two-thirds of all processed foods now contain corn in some form. Thus it is beyond the scope of this cookbook to indicate totally all sources of corn. Most corn sensitive individuals can tolerate the minute amount of corn which may be the starch in some brands of baking powder. With items that contain large amounts of corn, such as margarine, we have notated that food as corn containing. We have also designated corn syrup a corn product, even though the ingredient listing indicates this food is now mostly made from sugar.

*Sugar Reduced:* There are so many ways, reasons and methods to reduce or avoid sugar in the diet that a cookbook for each would be necessary. Basically we have tried to find sugar-reduced recipes and have included some recipes which use natural sweeteners such as fruit, honey or pure maple syrup. Other recipes use commercial sweeteners. Still others use sugar in very small quantity. Use the ones that fit your special needs or preferences.

*Additive/Salicylate Free:* This is not a Feingold cookbook, but we have marked some recipes A/S free or adaptive. Recipes so marked will be based on the Feingold restrictions of salicylate-containing fruits, vegetables, BHA/BHT, artificial color and flavor. A recipe calling for jello would not be marked, but if you have devised a good additive-free jello substitute, try it in the recipe. If the recipe contains an ingredient such as margarine, butter, oil or soy sauce, for example, we presume you can substitute a safe brand. (In using any commercial product, *be sure* that the product is allowed on your diet.)

This book does not promise miracles, but it does help you replace allergenic foods with products that taste as close to the original as possible. The breads will be tasty and nutritious, but they will not look or taste like the white bread available at the supermarket. The ice cream will be delicious and refreshing, but different from what you are accustomed to. Ask an established diabetic friend if he misses sugar; the answer will be "no." Taste adapts very quickly.

All these recipes have been tested and tasted before inclusion in this book. However, let me mention Hock, Stock and Barley Soup on p. 42. Two cooks prepared it and the results were entirely different. One soup sample did not include celery because of family sensitivity. Since this cook liked hearty soups, the vegetables were left in big chunks and the meat picked off the bones and returned to the soup. The second sample left out carrots because of family aversion. This cook liked smooth soup so the vegetables were puréed and the meat was left out. Both were great soups, but very different. And it would be different again if you left out the tomato because of the Feingold diet, or the split peas because of legume avoidance or the barley because of celiac disease. The outcome of any of these recipes will be at the mercy of diet limitations, family preferences, and personal style.

Finally, keep in mind that many food sensitivities are of short duration, usually six months or a year. Check by eating a food for a trial of three weeks. If no symptoms recur, you can expand your diet to include this food. Of course, this would not be true for individuals with intolerances. However, they can use the same techniques to experiment with their limits. For example, some people with lactose intolerance can manage the equivalent of 2-4 ounces of milk a day. Some with gluten intolerance can eat oats or wheat starch. Those with immediate food allergies to items such as nuts, shellfish and legumes should never experiment.

To further enlarge the number of recipes available to you, watch throughout the cookbook for the special tips which will enhance your cooking skills.

Now go ahead and cook up a storm. Bon appetit!

LEGEND

M = Milk-free          C = Corn-free
E = Egg-free           S = Sugar reduced
W = Wheat-free         F = Salicylate-free
G = Gluten-free        Y = Yeast-free

# Substitutes and Suggestions in Cooking

Besides using recipes from this cookbook, you may want to alter popular recipes to suit a medically prescribed diet. Many of your favorite recipes can be modified, though you may have to experiment several times with the recipe. Try it as written the first time and then judge if there should be more of one ingredient and less of another. This section provides ideas for substitutes under the headings: Egg, Milk, Wheat/Gluten, Sugar and Miscellaneous.

## Egg Free

Eggs function in baked products as a structural component, nutrient source, foam formation, flavor, and as a source of liquid. They hold a cooked product together. They add lightness when beaten to form air bubbles. In cookies, eggs serve mainly as a source of liquid, structure and nutritional quality. Structure does not seem to be severely affected by omitting eggs from the recipe as long as adequate liquid is added. Liquid may be replaced by adding three tablespoons of water for each egg omitted.

The nutrient quality contributed by the egg is more difficult to replace when it is omitted from a recipe. Cholesterol-free egg substitutes on the market cannot be used in egg-free recipes as they contain egg whites, the major source of egg allergen for most patients. To substitute nutritionally for protein and Vitamin B in eggs, use meat, fish, poultry, liver, cheese, dried beans or nuts.

Eggs act as a gelling agent in custards and cannot be eliminated from custard without the addition of some other agent such as gelatin. The lecithin in egg yolk also acts as an emulsifier for the fat in baked foods. In egg-free recipes the fat is often melted and boiled with the liquid and stirred quickly into the dry ingredients to effect good dispersion of water and fat phases. This procedure can, to some extent, take the place of the emulsifying action of the egg yolk.

1. Try the commercial egg replacer products available at some health food stores and gourmet shops. Directions for their use are printed on the package. These products are acceptable substitutes in recipes in which eggs are an important but not a

15

crucial ingredient. Such products are not a nutritive substitute for eggs.

2. Substitute for one egg: 2 tablespoons flour, ½ tablespoon shortening, ½ teaspoon baking powder, 2 tablespoons liquid.

3. Substitute for one egg: 2 tablespoons water, ½ teaspoon baking powder. This does especially well in cookie or cake recipes calling for only one egg.

4. Substitute for one egg: 1 tablespoon of vinegar for each egg required in baking, especially in cake mixes. Such baked goods should be eaten within 3 days.

5. Substitute for one egg: 1 teaspoon of baking powder for each egg needed in a cake mix.

6. Some of the loaf or bread-type mixes call for an egg, but make up well without one.

7. Some recipes call for only one or two eggs and a large quantity of baking powder or baking soda. This type of recipe could be tried without eggs as the relatively large amounts of baking powder and/or baking soda help make up for the volume that would have been produced by the eggs.

8. If you bake a cake without eggs, you may find the flavor change can be covered by increasing such ingredients as raisins or spices.

9. Beat an eggless cake more in between each mixture addition. Once the beating is complete, handle batter very gently and as little as possible. Bake immediately to prevent the escape of air.

10. If the recipe is milk free and wheat or gluten free, the baking process should be long and at a low temperature.

11. For eggless cookie recipes, grease the cookie sheet and lightly dust with flour. Floured cookie sheets help to keep cookies from spreading and losing their shape.

12. Read labels on baking powder cans carefully to note ingredients. Baking powder containing egg white should not be used in egg-free recipes.

## Milk Free

In baking, milk is used as a source of liquid and for flavor. It also adds nutrient quality to a product. In milk-free recipes water and fruit juices can be substituted as alternative sources of liquid. Nutrient quality can be enhanced by using a milk substitute such as soy milk, of which there are many brands on the market. These products have the approximate nutrient composition of whole milk when diluted as directed.

1. Liquid soy milk can be used in most recipes. If the recipe calls for 1 cup of whole milk, use ½ cup liquid soy milk and ½ cup water. If the recipe calls for evaporated milk, use an equal measure of soy milk as it comes from the can.

   If using powdered soy milk, reconstitute in the following amounts for use in recipes:

   > 1 tablespoon powder to ¼ cup water
   > 4 tablespoons powder to 1 cup water
   > 4 teaspoons powder to ⅓ cup water

   If using liquid milk, reconstitute by mixing together equal parts of water and undiluted liquid soy milk.

2. Goat's milk is available in powder, can or fresh at some health food or gourmet stores.

3. Products marked "parve" do not contain milk or milk products.

4. Coconut milk can be made from 1 cup fresh coconut or 1 cup coconut meal and 2 cups water. Whip in blender until smooth. Store covered in refrigerator.

5. If a small amount of milk is called for, try an equal amount of water or fruit juice, or meat or vegetable stock, or water plus 1½ teaspoons of milk-free margarine or oil.

6. Use vegetable oil or French or Italian Dressing instead of butter on vegetables.

7. Use soy milk such as Mullsoy, Nutramigen or Isomil in coffee and tea.

8. Use milk-free margarine instead of butter in recipes.

9. Instead of whipped cream, look for a commercial whipped topping that is milk free.

10. So-called milk substitutes often contain sodium caseinate which is often the allergic factor of milk (though sodium caseinate is safe for lactose-free diets). Read ingredients on such packages.

11. If you find the taste of soy milk unpleasant, add a teaspoonful of lime juice to a large glass. The lime cannot be detected and overcomes the strong soy flavor.

12. When making rolls and bread, use potato water in place of milk.

13. Tapioca and rice puddings can be made with fruit juice.

14. When a recipe calls for cream of mushroom soup, substitute a can of chicken gumbo soup (gluten and milk free) and a small can of sliced mushrooms.

15. For creamy mashed potatoes, use white potatoes which have been well-cooked, drain thoroughly, add milk-free margarine and seasonings, then mash. Add ½ – 1 teaspoon baking powder per cup of mashed potatoes to make them light and fluffy.

16. A child on a milk-free diet can feel a bit left out when the gang starts drinking hot chocolate. Try serving Hot Tang (quick and good), rose hip tea or any mild herb tea.

17. Use extra sandwich fillings to provide moisture to unbuttered bread.

18. For frying, use oil or bacon fat.

19. When using fruit juice or fruit purée instead of milk, the finished product may not be as rich tasting.

20. If the recipe calls for yeast or baking powder, work very quickly so the fruit will not neutralize the rising action of these leavening agents.

21. Fresh soy bean curd mixed with fruit makes a good substitute for cottage cheese.

22. Tofu, a form of soy bean curd, makes an acceptable substitute for cheese, especially in cooking.

23. For 1 cup sour cream in recipes, stir 4 tablespoons of allowed starch into ¾ cup water and ¼ cup of vinegar.

A child between 3 and 16 years old should, so nutritionists say, have about 700 mg of calcium per day. Eight ounces of milk provides 290 mg. The following are suggested replacements in descending order of value:

| | |
|---|---|
| ½ cup salmon plus bones | 320 mg |
| ½ cup green leaf vegetables | 140 mg |
| artichoke | 100 mg |
| ⅔ cup broccoli or ½ cup canned beans | 80 mg |
| orange or ⅔ cup cooked beans or ½ cup | |
|     lima beans or ½ cup parsnips | 50 mg |
| egg | 25 mg |
| slice of whole wheat bread or 1 tablespoon | |
|     peanut butter or ½ cup peas | 20 mg |

Do not forget to supplement Vitamin D when milk is removed from the diet. The calcium found in fish is absorbed just as readily as that found in milk. (Salt water canned fish is relatively uncontaminated by chemicals.) Remember that proper calcium absorption requires Vitamin D (the sunshine vitamin) and fish oil is an excellent source of Vitamin D. Vitamin D is also necessary for us to utilize the calcium stores in our bones and teeth when the calcium level in the blood is reduced during vigorous exercise. Since millions of adults do not receive sun on their skin for several months during the winter, a Vitamin D supplement is essential for them to maintain good health until the spring days stretch beyond office hours.

## Milk Free Calcium Supplements:

*Canada*   Calcium Sandoz Syrup
           Calcium Sandoz Forte (effervescent tablets)
           Calcium Gluconate
           Bone Meal and Dolomite—natural sources available in
               health food store
           Gramcal (effervescent tablets)

*U.S.A.*   Neo-calglucon
           Glubionate Calcium Syrup (same formula as Calcium
               Sandoz)
           HCS bone meal with Vitamins A & D.

Lactic acid is required to retain desirable bacterial balance in the intestines. Those allergic to milk or lacking the enzyme to digest lactose, can obtain lactic acid from cider vinegar or sauerkraut. Following a dose of antibiotics (which kills off the good bacteria with the bad), a serving of sauerkraut should help get things back in balance.

For those allergic to milk and corn, an excellent calcium supplement is Dolomite, available in health food stores. Bone meal tablets are possibly the most easily absorbed source of calcium supplement. If a calcium supplement bothers digestion, put it in a glass of juice to dilute the concentration of the base.

## Wheat Free and Gluten Free

Wheat is the aristocrat among grains because it contains more of a rather gluey protein called gluten. The carbon dioxide gas produced by the yeast or other leavening agent in bread and baking blows up the loaf or cake, but the tough, elastic gluten holds it together. Rye, barley, oats, corn, millet or buckwheat will not make a light, spongy loaf or baked product. Grain foods all contain starch and a fair amount of protein. Depending on the form in which we eat cereal, some are valuable sources of thiamine and iron.

The following flours and meals may be substituted for 1 cup of wheat flour:

For Wheat-free Diets:
| | | |
|---|---:|---:|
| ½ cup barley flour | | 125 mL |
| 1¼ cups rye flour | | 310 mL |
| 1 cup rye meal | | 250 mL |
| 1⅓ cups ground rolled oats | | 325 mL |
| ½ cup rye flour and ½ cup potato flour | 125 mL | 125 mL |
| ⅔ cup rye flour and ⅓ cup potato flour | 150 mL | 75 mL |
| ⅝ cup rice flour and ⅓ cup rye flour | 140 mL | 75 mL |

All combinations of gluten-free diet suggestions except wheat starch

For Gluten-free Diets:

| | |
|---|---|
| 1 cup corn flour | 250 mL |
| ¾ cup coarse corn meal | 195 mL |
| 1 scant cup of fine corn meal | 240 mL |
| ⅝ cup potato flour (sometimes called potato starch) | 140 mL |
| 1 scant cup wheat starch | 240 mL |
| ⅞ cup rice flour | 225 mL |
| ⅝ cup rice flour and ⅓ cup potato flour | 140 mL 75 mL |
| 1 cup soy flour and ¾ cup potato flour | 250 mL 200 mL |

## *Gluten-Free Flour Mix*

This can be kept on hand for use for substituting directly into any recipe calling for all-purpose wheat flour. If recipe calls for 1 cup (250 mL) of flour, use 1 cup (250 mL) of mix.

Sift together six times:

| | |
|---|---|
| 2 cups wheat starch | 500 mL |
| ¾ cup potato flour | 195 mL |
| ¾ cup corn flour | 195 mL |
| ¼ cup soy flour | 60 mL |
| 1 cup rice flour | 250 mL |
| 6 tablespoons arrowroot flour | 100 mL |
| 6 tablespoons tapioca flour | 100 mL |

Store in an airtight container.

If you use this combination for baking, the time should be longer and the oven cooler than the original recipe calls for.

Blend together thoroughly. Use this in any recipe calling for all-purpose flour *except* bread, gingerbread, doughnuts, fritters or shortbread, unless you have a special gluten-free recipe.

1. Coarser meals and gluten-free or wheat-free flours need more leavening. It is advisable to use 2½ teaspoons (12 mL) of baking powder to each cup of coarse flour.

2. Never use soy flour alone; always use it in combination with another flour.

3. When using gluten-free flour especially, let the dough sit for ½-1 hour or overnight in the refrigerator. This softens it and produces a better finished product.

4. Look for recipes which use a small amount of wheat flour in combination with another type of flour, such as cornmeal or oatmeal. It is easier then to substitute another flour for the wheat flour.

5. To avoid graininess in rice flour and cornmeal, mix with the liquid in recipe, bring to a boil and cool before mixing with other ingredients.

6. Recipes calling for cake flours are especially adaptable since they usually do not depend upon gluten for their structure.

7. If using celimix, try substituting ½ cup (125 mL) arrowroot flour or ½ cup (125 mL) buckwheat flour in place of ½ cup (125 mL) of the mix, then just use the recipe as per package directions. This makes a less crumbly loaf.

8. Keep non-wheat baked products in the refrigerator to lessen crumbliness.

9. Some cookie and cake recipes can take unsifted rice flour substituted directly into the recipe.

10. To make rice flour cakes more moist add a synthetic whipped cream powder to the dry ingredients and increase the liquid until the batter is "wet" enough.

11. Use gelatin as a binder in breads. It works well in rice flour recipes. Soften the gelatin in half the water the recipe calls for, then heat it just enough to dissolve the gelatin. Then add the gelatin mixture to the rest of the liquid and finish the recipe.

12. Fill the smaller (neck) end of your turkey with stuffing made from allergen-free bread for the allergic member of the household.

13. Binder for meat loaf and meat patties can be made of rice flour, or 1 cup puffed rice to 1 pound of ground meat, or an egg, or instant mashed potatoes.

14. Recipes not containing wheat need long, slow baking, especially if egg and milk are not used.

15. For cookies, mix wheat starch and soy flour in any proportion in the quantity called for in the original recipe.

16. Use your own allowed granola mix to replace nuts and give crunchiness to cookies.

17. In recipes calling for milk or water, heat these liquids slightly before adding to dry ingredients. Shortening may also be melted in this warm liquid which will cut down on mixing time.

18. For bread recipes, double the amounts called for and make several small loaves. They freeze well. Since the loaves dry out in about two days, cut your loaves into pieces before freezing and defrost these as needed.

19. Use crushed cornflakes or crisp rice cereals for crumbing foods or in desserts such as apple crisps and pie crusts. Use potato chips for casseroles.

20. A banana blends ingredients together well.

21. Batters made from flours other than wheat may appear much thinner or much thicker than batters made from wheat flours.

22. Cakes made with substitute flours other than wheat tend to be dry. The moisture can be preserved by icing the cake or by storing them tightly covered.

23. Meat cookies can be quickly made by just mixing a jar of baby meat with rice or other pablum, and adding ½ teaspoon baking powder. Bake in moderate oven about 10 minutes.

24. For thickening sauces, gravies or puddings, substitute one of the following for 1 tablespoon wheat flour:

| | |
|---|---|
| ½ tablespoon cornstarch | 8 mL |
| ½ tablespoon potato starch flour | 8 mL |
| ½ tablespoon rice starch | 8 mL |
| ½ tablespoon arrowroot starch | 8 mL |
| 2 teaspoons quick-cooking tapioca | 10 mL |
| 2 teaspoons tapioca flour | 10 mL |

25. Wheat-free spaghetti and noodles are available in specialty stores. Chinese bean threads are an acceptable substitute for spaghetti, as is spaghetti squash.

26. An equal amount of frozen French fries may be substituted in a

casserole to replace macaroni, spaghetti or noodles.

27. To bread fish, chops and chicken, dip meat into rice flour, diluted evaporated milk, then into allowed crumbs. Refrigerate one hour before cooking.

28. You can make your own "breading" mixture. Mix 1 cup ( 250 mL) of recommended flour, 1 cup (250 mL) allowed bread-crumbs, 1 teaspoon (5 mL) seasoned salt, ¼ teaspoon (1 mL) pepper, ¼ teaspoon (1 mL) spice (sage for chicken, thyme for pork, tarragon for fish). Keep in plastic bags in the refrigerator.

29. Hold meat together in patties or meat loaf with cooked oat-meal, grated nuts or potato.

$$1 \text{ cup (250 mL) flour} = \text{¾ cup (195 mL) cornmeal or ½ cup (125 mL) oatmeal}$$
$$1 \text{ tablespoon (15 mL) flour} = \text{½ tablespoon (25 mL) starch}$$

## Sugar Free

Sugar is an essential ingredient in traditional baking. Besides con-tributing a sweet taste, sugar causes browning, initiates the action of yeast, helps increase the size of cakes and makes baked goods more tender.

Sugar can be made from cane or beet, and comes in several forms besides the usual granulated form. Icing sugar, sometimes known as powdered or confectioner's sugar, is sifted sugar and contains corn or wheat starch or corn flour to keep it free flowing. Berry or castor sugar is finely granulated so it can be used in a shaker on shortbread or fruit. Party sugar comes in large granules and is sometimes artificially coloured for special effect in the sugar bowl. Brown sugar is color-graded by names: light yellow, golden brown, old-fashioned, or dark. Demerara sugar is a coarse brown sugar with a slight rum flavor. Molasses is a by-product of sugar refining. Sorghum is made from sorghum grass and is thinner than molasses and has a slightly more sour flavor.

Not all recipes lend themselves to substituting sugar. This is a suggested list of equivalent substitutes for one cup of white or brown sugar:

¾ cup (195 mL) maple syrup and reduce the liquid called for by 2 tablespoons (30 mL).

1 cup (250 mL) honey and reduce liquid called for by ¼ cup (50 mL).

1 cup (250 mL) molasses and reduce liquid called for by ½ cup (50 mL) and add ½ teaspoon (2 mL) baking powder.

1½ cups (375 mL) sorghum and reduce liquid called for by ½ cup (50 mL).

1 cup (250 mL) corn syrup (if pure) and reduce liquid called for by ½ cup (125 mL).

1. When a liquid is substituted in a recipe for sugar, omit ½ or ¼ cup (125 mL or 50 mL) of the liquid specified in the recipe. If your diet allows, only substitute half the sugar for the liquid sweetener. This is especially helpful when baking with rye and oat flours. Leave baking a day to develop a better flavor.

2. For those with disaccharide intolerance, sucrose-free baby formulas can be used as a milk-like drink.

3. Goat's milk combined with sucrose-free soy milk makes a richer cooked product.

4. Aspartame (trade name Equal) can be substituted sparingly for sugar for table top use. It does not work in the heating process.

5. Use the juice from unsweetened fruit such as pineapple or fruits packed in pear juice instead of a sugar syrup.

6. Consider eliminating sugar in June and July if you are allergic to grass, as cane sugar and grass are related botanically.

7. Club soda contains no sweetening and makes a refreshing drink if you add peppermint, rum or raspberry flavorings.

People with hypoglycemia (low blood sugar) must not use any of the above sweeteners. Instead, they must use artificial sweeteners in liquid, granulated or tablet form.

Liquid equivalents:

| Liquid | | Sugar | |
|---|---|---|---|
| ¼ teaspoon | 1 mL | 2 teaspoons | 10 mL |
| 1 teaspoon | 5 mL | 8 teaspoons | 40 mL |

| 2 teaspoons | 10 mL | ⅓ cup | 75 mL |
| 1 tablespoon | 5 mL | ½ cup | 125 mL |

Tablet equivalent:

¼ g  =  1 teaspoon sugar

½ g  =  2 teaspoons sugar

Be sure to check labels for other allergens. Some brands are not milk free. When using artificial sweeteners, be careful not to add too much or your food will have a bitter taste. It is best to start off with a very small amount of sweetener and increase it next time, if necessary. Tablets are cheaper than liquid, but liquid is less bitter for cooking. When possible, add the sweetener *after* cooking (i.e., for rhubarb or applesauce).

Remember that ordinary sugar preserves, adds bulk, stabilizes and sweetens, whereas artificial sweeteners merely sweeten. When replacing sugar with artificial sweeteners (especially a large quantity such as ½ cup [125 mL]), you must adjust the other ingredients to make up for the loss of the sugar properties.

Cereal, fruit and decaffeinated coffee, which usually call for a little sugar, can with perseverance, be enjoyed without any sweetener at all.

Anyone with hypoglycemia can carry gelatin capsules when away from home. They provide protein when a snack is impossible to obtain. Keep them by your bedside and take during the night if you wake up with any low blood sugar symptoms. Capsules are available at drug stores.

## Miscellaneous

1. For spice allergies, simply omit the spice in question. The same is true for herbs and mustard.

2. To substitute for semi-sweet chocolate or chocolate morsels (which may contain gluten) in a recipe, use 2 level tablespoons of cocoa and 2 level tablespoons of butter, margarine or shortening for each one ounce square of chocolate called for in the recipe.

3. For those allergic to gluten or soy products, make your own soy sauce by experimenting with salt, hot water, molasses or caramel. The flavor is affected by the heat of the water.

4. Canned junior meats make a handy sandwich filling either on bread or bread substitute.

5. Adding mashed bananas to mixtures in which there have been substitutions helps hold the mixture together and also adds flavor.

6. Tapioca is very well tolerated by persons with food allergies. To Minute Tapioca and soy milk, add a little vanilla and sugar, cook to pudding form, then add a little corn syrup on top.

7. Ground lamb can be just as versatile as beef. Use to make hamburgers, shepherd's pie, meat loaf. Not all stores will grind lamb for you. When you convince one to do so, have them put a bit of lamb fat through the grinder first. This removes all traces of any other meat ground previously. Don't forget that lamb livers and kidneys can be used to provide variety. A good sandwich spread can be made by grinding up liver with whatever else can be tolerated and moistened with soy milk substitute. Also, one kidney and one liver ground into 10 pounds of meat yields a delicious, nutritious variation.

8. Use carob powder in recipes in place of chocolate or cocoa by equal substitution. Carob looks like chocolate or cocoa and can be purchased at health food stores.

9. If you are unable to use lemon juice or ascorbic acid to prevent discoloration of fruit, a mild salt solution will do the job.

10. Baking powder may contain corn so check the ingredient listing on the container carefully. A drug store will make up substitute baking powder. It is possible to substitute 1 teaspoon baking powder for 1 egg in quick-bread recipes, but do not use this substitute in cake recipes.

11. The content of corn in baking powder is so infinitesimal that most tartrate baking powders are acceptable, except in extremely unusual cases. The following is a corn-free baking powder:

> 1 part baking soda
> 1 part cream of tartar
> 1 part potato starch

Make up in any quantity and substitute directly.

12. Sometimes merely using equal amounts of cream of tartar and baking soda is sufficient, especially for heavy batters such as Christmas cake. For example, if the recipe calls for 1 teaspoon baking powder, use 1 teaspoon cream of tartar and 1 teaspoon of baking soda.

## Some General Suggestions

1. Batters adjusted with substitutions may remain runny, so bake in a pan with a rim to protect your oven; do not fill to the top.

2. Cakes which have been made with substitutes are very delicate. For easier removal, grease pan, line with waxed paper, grease and flour the waxed paper with allowed substitutes for the grease and flour.

3. Always be on the lookout for recipes that do not use the allergenic food, or that need so little of the allergenic food that substitution is easy.

4. When cooking for allergic children, think of their food in terms of substitutes for the ordinary food the rest of the family is having. The closer in appearance an allergic child's food looks to the family food, the more satisfied and appreciative he will be. This is even more important when a child goes to a party. Most hostesses are very cooperative about their menu, so that you can match the food served as nearly as possible with your child's special foods.

5. Be creative. If you can't use a traditional birthday cake, invent one—either a mock one out of cardboard or say, a brick of ice cream, frosted with whipping cream and drizzled with chocolate sauce, topped by lighted candles.

6. Look into Chinese wok cookery or East Indian cooking as these do not use traditional North American and European ingredients.

# BREAKFASTS

Breakfast can be a tricky meal. Unless you are the type who wakes up ready and ravenous, your appetite probably has to be tempted. In any case, breakfast is an important meal and should be as nutritious as possible. If you and members of your family run through the kitchen, grab a handful of whatever is available and take off for the day, breakfast obviously has to be quick as well.

This section includes cereals, muffins, pancakes and waffles, but there is no reason to stick to these. Let your tastebuds and imagination roam.

**Free of: E**

**Can be free of: M W G C F S**

## Granola Cereal

| | | | | |
|---|---|---|---|---|
| 8 cups rolled oats (*G) | 2 L | 1 cup lecithin granules | 250 mL |
| 1 cup unsalted raw sunflower seeds | 250 mL | 1 teaspoon salt | 5 mL |
| 1 cup sesame seeds or flax seeds | 250 mL | ½ cup powdered skim milk (optional) (*M) | 125 mL |
| 1 cup sliced almonds (*F) or other nuts (optional) | 250 mL | 1 cup vegetable oil (*C, F) | 250 mL |
| 1 cup raw wheat germ (*G) or corn grits (*C) | 250 mL | 1 cup liquid honey, corn syrup (*S, C) or maple syrup | 250 mL |
| 1 cup dessicated coconut (preferably unsweetened) *or* | 250 mL | 2 cups raisins or currants (*F) (optional) | 500 mL |

Mix dry ingredients thoroughly (do not add raisins). Blend in oil and honey. Bake on broiler tray at 250°F (120°C) for 1½ hours, stirring every half hour. Add raisins after cooking, while still warm. If you use salted sunflower seeds, do not add extra salt. Delicious with milk or serve dry for snacks.

| Free of: E W |
| --- |
| Can be free of: M G F |
| Contains: C S |

# Breakfast Bars

⅓ cup melted butter or 75 mL
  milk-free margarine (*M,F)
2 cups quick-cooking 500 mL
  oats (*G)
½ teaspoon salt 2 mL

½ cup brown sugar 100 mL
¼ cup corn syrup (*F) 50 mL
1½ teaspoons vanilla 7 mL
½ cup chopped nuts 125 mL
  (optional)

Combine butter and oats. Add next five ingredients. Pack very firmly in a well-greased, shallow 7 inch × 11 inch (17 cm × 27 cm) baking pan. Bake at 400°F (200°C) for 12 minutes. (Do not overbake or bars will become very hard.) Cool slightly, then cut into 48 bars. Refrigerate to harden.

| Free of: E W G C S |
| --- |
| Contains: M F |

# Breakfast Rice

Makes 4 servings

A great breakfast for a rice lover.

1 cup brown rice 250 mL
4 cups milk 1 L

1 cup raisins 250 mL
  Maple syrup or honey

Grind the rice in an electric blender until the kernels are half the original size. Combine rice with milk and raisins in a saucepan. Bring to a boil, cover and simmer until rice is cooked, about 10–15 minutes. Serve with syrup or honey.

## Variations
Add dates, apricots or figs. Nuts are also delicious.

Free of: E W G C S

Can be free of: F

Contains: M

# Millet with Cheese

Makes 4 servings

| | | | |
|---|---|---|---|
| ½ cup millet | 125 mL | 2 tablespoons butter (*F) | 25 mL |
| 1½ cups water or milk | 375 mL | | |
| Salt to taste | | 1 cup grated cheese (*F) | 250 mL |

Combine millet, water and salt in a saucepan. Bring to a boil, cover and simmer for 30 minutes.

Place millet mixture in pan with melted butter and ½ cup cheese. Heat, stirring constantly until the cheese melts. Sprinkle with the remainder of the cheese and serve.

Free of: M E W G

Can be free of: F

Contains: C S

# Corn and Rice Muffins

Makes 6 small muffins

| | | | |
|---|---|---|---|
| ½ cup rice flour | 125 mL | 2 tablespoons sugar | 25 mL |
| ½ cup corn meal | 125 mL | ½ cup water | 125 mL |
| ½ teaspoon salt | 2 mL | 2 tablespoons melted shortening (*F) | 25 mL |
| 2 teaspoons baking powder | 10 mL | | |

Preheat oven to 400°F (200°C). Mix and sift dry ingredients. Stir in water and shortening and beat until very well blended. Bake in small, greased muffin pans for 25 minutes. Delicious with cheese if milk is tolerated.

| Can be free of: M G C F |
|---|
| Contains: E W S |

# Date Muffins

| | | | | |
|---|---|---|---|---|
| 1 cup chopped dates | 250 mL | | ⅓ cup rice flour | 75 mL |
| 1 teaspoon baking soda | 5 mL | | 1 teaspoon baking powder | 5 mL |
| ¾ cup boiling water | 175 mL | | ¼ cup melted butter (or oil) (*C, M, F) | 50 mL |
| 1 egg | | | | |
| ¾ cup brown sugar | 175 mL | | ¾ cup chopped walnuts | 175 mL |
| 1 teaspoon vanilla | 5 mL | | | |
| 1 teaspoon salt | 5 mL | | | |
| 1 cup wheat starch flour (*G) | 250 mL | | | |

Place finely chopped dates in a bowl and add soda and boiling water. Mix and let stand until cool. Gradually add sugar to beaten egg, then add vanilla and salt. Combine with date mixture. Combine flours and baking powder and add to mixture. Add cooled melted butter, nuts and mix. Spoon into well-greased muffin pans. Bake at 350°F (180°C) for 15 minutes.

## Variation
Pour into a greased 9 inch × 5 inch (23 cm × 12 cm) loaf pan and bake at 350°F (180°C) for 40 minutes.

| Free of: W S |
|---|
| Can be free of: M G C F |
| Contains: E |

# Oat Muffins

Makes 6 muffins

| | | | | |
|---|---|---|---|---|
| 1 cup sifted oat flour (*G) | 250 mL | | ¼ cup cold water or milk (*M) | 50 mL |
| ½ teaspoon salt | 2 mL | | 1 egg, well beaten | |
| 2½ teaspoons baking powder | 12 mL | | 2 tablespoons butter or milk-free margarine (*C, F) | 25 mL |
| 8 drops artificial sweetener | | | | |

Preheat oven to 425°F (220°C). In a bowl, combine oat flour, salt and baking powder. Add sweetener, milk, egg and butter. Mix only to blend. Pour into greased muffin tins. Bake for 25 minutes. Recipe may be doubled.

## *Pineapple Rye Muffins*

Makes 6 muffins

| | | | |
|---|---|---|---|
| 1½ cups rye flour | 375 mL | 1 egg | |
| ½ teaspoon salt | 2 mL | ½ cup water or | 125 mL |
| 4 tablespoons sugar | 50 mL | pineapple juice | |
| 5 teaspoons baking powder | 25 mL | 4 tablespoons fat, melted | 50 mL |
| 4 tablespoons crushed pineapple, drained | 50 mL | | |

Preheat oven to 400°F (200°C). Sift dry ingredients; add drained crushed pineapple. Combine beaten egg, water and melted fat. Add to dry ingredients and stir just until moistened. (Mixture will have lumpy appearance.) Fill greased muffin pans ⅔ full, handling the batter as little as possible. Bake for 35 minutes.

## *Rice and Barley Cereal Muffins*

Makes 6 muffins

| | | | |
|---|---|---|---|
| ⅓ cup rice flour | 75 mL | 1 tablespoon oil (*C, F) | 15 mL |
| ⅓ cup barley cereal | 75 mL | ½ cup water | 125 mL |
| 6 tablespoons sugar | 75 mL | | |
| ¼ teaspoon salt | 1 mL | | |
| 4 teaspoons baking powder | 20 mL | | |

Preheat oven to 400°F (200°C). Sift and mix the dry ingredients; add the oil and water. Pour into well-greased muffin tins. Bake for 35 minutes.

| Free of: M E W G |
| --- |
| Can be free of: C F |
| Contains: S |

# Rice Flour and Peanut Butter Muffins

Makes 6 muffins

| | | | |
| --- | --- | --- | --- |
| 1 cup rice flour | 250 mL | 1 tablespoon oil (*C, F) | 15 mL |
| 4 teaspoons baking powder | 20 mL | ½ cup water | 125 mL |
| ¼ teaspoon salt | 1 mL | 3 teaspoons peanut butter (*C, F) | 15 mL |
| 2 tablespoons sugar | 25 mL | | |

Preheat oven to 425°F (220°C). Sift dry ingredients together. Add oil, water and peanut butter. Mix. Fill muffin tins, greased with oil, ⅔ full. Bake for about 20 minutes.

| Free of: M E W G |
| --- |
| Can be free of: C F |
| Contains: S |

# Rice Flour Banana Muffins

Very good and versatile.

| | | | |
| --- | --- | --- | --- |
| 1 cup mashed banana | 250 mL | ¼ teaspoon salt | 1 mL |
| ¼ cup melted shortening (*C, F) | 50 mL | ½ teaspoon baking soda | 2 mL |
| ¾ cup white sugar (can use only ½ cup) | 175 mL | 1¼ cups plus 2 tablespoons rice flour | 300 mL |
| ½ teaspoon vanilla | 2 mL | 2 teaspoons baking powder | 10 mL |

Blend banana, shortening, sugar and vanilla. Add dry ingredients unsifted. Bake for 25 minutes at 375°F (190°C) in greased muffin tins.

**Note:** Honey can be substituted for sugar if more flour is added to compensate for liquid.

## *Variations*
Add any of the following to muffin batters:

| | |
|---|---|
| ¼ cup fresh berries or cherries | 60 mL |
| ⅓ cup cubed raw apple | 75 mL |
| ¼ cup raisins or dates | 60 mL |
| ⅓ cup cubed banana | 75 mL |

You can also sprinkle sugar and cinnamon on top of unbaked muffins. Or put a few nuts and 1 teaspoon (5 mL) brown sugar on the bottom of each muffin pan and pour batter on top. You might also try sprinkling a few sesame seeds on top of the unbaked muffins.

Free of: W G C S

Can be free of: M F

Contains: E

# *Rice Griddle Cakes*

| | | | |
|---|---|---|---|
| 1 egg | | 1½ cups cooked rice | 375 mL |
| ¼ cup grated cheese (optional) (*M, F) | 50 mL | Salt, pepper, to taste | |

Beat egg and cheese into rice. Season with salt and pepper. Shape rice into small flat cakes and fry in a greased skillet. Brown thoroughly on each side and serve hot.

# Buckwheat Pancakes

Makes 10 large or 20 small pancakes

| | | | |
|---|---|---|---|
| 2 cups lukewarm water | 500 mL | ½ cup potato flour | 125 mL |
| 1 tablespoon dry active yeast | 15 mL | ½ cup rice flour | 125 mL |
| | | 1 cup milk, scalded and cooled | 250 mL |
| 2 tablespoons brown sugar | 25 mL | 1 teaspoon salt | 5 mL |
| 2 cups buckwheat flour | 500 mL | | |

Mix together warm water, yeast and sugar. Stir in buckwheat flour, potato flour and rice flour. Stir in milk and salt. Cover and set in warm place to rise for 1 hour. Stir well and bake on hot griddle.

## Variation
Use 1 cup (250 mL) wheat flour in place of potato and rice flour.

# Cottage Cheese Pancakes

| | | | |
|---|---|---|---|
| 1 cup cottage cheese | 250 mL | ¼ cup rice flour | 60 mL |
| 2 eggs, lightly beaten | | ¼ teaspoon baking powder | 1 mL |
| 2 tablespoons potato flour | 25 mL | 1 tablespoon melted butter (*F) | 15 mL |

Mix together cottage cheese, eggs, flours, baking powder and butter. Fry on a hot, oiled griddle. Delicious served with apple sauce.

# Potato Pancakes

Makes 10 pancakes

Free of: W G

Can be free of: S C F

Contains: M E

| | | | | |
|---|---|---|---|---|
| 1 beaten egg | | ½ cup instant | 125 mL |
| 1 cup buttermilk | 250 mL | potato flakes | |
| 1 tablespoon | 15 mL | ½ teaspoon baking | 2 mL |
| vegetable oil (*C, F) | | powder | |
| 1 tablespoon honey | 15 mL | ¾ cup potato flour | 175 mL |
| or brown sugar (*S) | | ¼ cup rice flour | 60 mL |

Beat eggs. Add buttermilk slowly, then oil and honey. Beat in the instant potato flakes. Add baking powder and potato and rice flours. Mix together. Fry on hot, oiled griddle until each side is golden.

Free of: W G C F

Can be free of: S

Contains: M E

# Rice Pancakes

| | | | | |
|---|---|---|---|---|
| 2 eggs | | ½ teaspoon salt | 2 mL |
| 1¼ cups buttermilk | 300 mL | 1½ teaspoons baking | 6 mL |
| ¾ cup rice flour | 175 mL | powder | |
| 1 tablespoon sugar | 15 mL | | |
| (*S) | | | |

Beat eggs and add half the buttermilk. Stir in sifted dry ingredients and add remainder of buttermilk. Let stand for 15 minutes to soften the rice flour. Fry on a hot, oiled griddle.

Free of: M E W G C F

Contains: S

# Rice-Potato Pancake Mix

| | | | |
|---|---|---|---|
| 1 cup rice flour | 250 mL | 1 teaspoon baking powder | 5 mL |
| ⅔ cup potato flour | 150 mL | | |
| ½ teaspoon salt | 2 mL | Water (or milk if allowed) | |
| 8 teaspoons white sugar | 40 mL | | |

Stir dry ingredients together. Stir together equal amounts of mix and liquid. Fry on a hot, oiled griddle.

This mix can be made up in large quantities by doubling or tripling recipe. Store in an airtight container. When needed, mix about 1 cup (250 mL) liquid with 1 cup (250 mL) of mix. This amount yields about 6 pancakes.

# LUNCHES

Lunches are the most difficult meal to cope with on a limited diet. Gluten-free (wheat, oats, barley and rye) bread is difficult to make sandwiches with, and many people find it unsuitable for packed lunches. It is easier to carry a piece of bread with margarine, a green salad, a hard-boiled egg, and some fruit. Rice crackers or special muffins carry well, and so does banana bread, which is more moist and less crumbly. Another hint is to toast the bread, butter it, and put in the filling, but let it cool two minutes before wrapping. (Use plastic wrap, rather than waxed paper.) Taco shells filled with cold meat also make a good lunch.

Wide-necked thermal jars can be very useful for those who carry a lunch pail. Interesting concoctions that are suitable for special diets—hearty homemade soups, stews or casseroles—can be carried and eaten right from the thermos. A beverage and fruit complete a good lunch. Just make sure there is variety as well as nutritional value.

Free of: M E W G

Can be free of: C F

Contains: S

## Cole Slaw

1 medium-sized
  cabbage, shredded
1 onion, grated
3 carrots, grated
1 green pepper, slivered

### Dressing

| | | |
|---|---|---|
| ½ cup white sugar | 125 mL |
| 1 teaspoon salt | 5 mL |
| ⅓ cup salad oil (*C, F) | 75 mL |
| ¾ cup vinegar | 175 mL |

Bring dressing ingredients to boil and pour over vegetables. Pack in large glass container. Refrigerate for 24 hours before serving. Will keep for 2–3 weeks.

Free of: M E W G C S F

# Non-Peanut Nut Butter

| | | | |
|---|---|---|---|
| 6 tablespoons of a tolerated oil (or water) Salt to taste | 100 mL | 1 cup of any tolerated seed or nut | 250 mL |

Place all ingredients in a blender and whiz until desired consistency.

Free of: W G C

Can be free of: M S

Contains: E F

# Meatza Pizza Pie

| | | | |
|---|---|---|---|
| 10 ounces tomato mixture* | 284 g | ¼ cup canned milk (*M) or soy milk undiluted | 60 mL |
| 1 pound ground beef | 500 g | ½ onion | |
| ½ cup milk-free instant mashed potatoes | 125 mL | 1 egg | |
| | | 1 teaspoon oregano | 5 mL |
| | | 1 teaspoon garlic salt | 5 mL |
| *or* | | Salt and pepper | |
| ¼ cup instant potato flakes (contain milk) (*M) | 60 mL | Mozzarella cheese (*M), mushrooms, salami and olives, if allowed | |

Prepare the tomato mixture of your choice. Mix the meat, potatoes, milk, onion, egg and spices well with 5 ounces (140 g) of prepared tomato mixture. Place in a 9 inch (23 cm) pie plate or two 8 inch (20 cm) pie plates and spread evenly over bottom.

Fill centre with remaining 5 ounces (140 g) of tomato mixture. Top with Mozzarella cheese, mushrooms, salami and olives. Bake at 350°F (180°C) for 30 minutes or until brown.

*Substitute: 1 can of tomato soup (not gluten or wheat free) or 10 ounces (284 g) mixture of tomato ketchup (*S) and tomato juice, or 10 ounces (284 g) mixture of tomato paste and tomato juice. Any of these three substitutes can be seasoned with such spices as dried onion, celery salt, seasoning salt, or parsley.

Free of: E W G C S

Can be free of: F

Contains: M

# Lactose-Free Cheese Spread

| ½ cup water | 125 mL | ¾ pound Cheddar | 340 g |
| 1 teaspoon lecithin (optional) | 5 mL | cheese (*F) | |

Whip ingredients in a blender or a food processor. Scrape into a jar or serving container and refrigerate until necessary.

## Soup Suggestions

*Meats:* Beef and poultry are good meats for soups, but lamb should be used sparingly as it has a strong flavor. Pork is too sweet to make good soup.

*Filler:* There are many ingredients which make soups heartier—try any one of rice, potato, beans, barley, lentils, peas or noodles.

*Vegetables:* Tomatoes, both canned and fresh, onions, parsnips, leeks, or celery make good soup. Turnips, broccoli stems and lima beans should be used sparingly because of strong flavor. Peas, corn and carrots are too sweet to be used alone.

*Thickening:* Add the following per 1 cup (250 mL) of soup liquid.

| 1 teaspoon barley | 5 mL |
| 1 teaspoon rice | 5 mL |
| 1 teaspoon oatmeal | 5 mL |
| 2 tablespoons wheat germ | 25 mL |

| | |
|---|---|
| 2 tablespoons soya flour | 25 mL |
| 1½ teaspoons flour | 7 mL |

These work best when mixed in cold water and then added to the soup. Leftover gravy is an excellent soup thickener.

*Seasonings:* Salt, pepper and a selection of peppercorns, paprika, thyme, bayleaf, barley, cayenne, mace or allspice are generally used in seasoning soups. Season lightly in the beginning, adding more seasoning immediately before serving.

Soup is best one day old when its flavor has intensified. Grease forms a cake that is easily removed from cold soup.

Free of: M E C S

Can be free of: W F

Contains: G

# Hock, Stock and Barley Soup

A very hearty soup.

| | | | |
|---|---|---|---|
| 2 pounds soup bones | 1000 g | 2 carrots, chopped | |
| ½ cup split peas | 125 mL | ¼ cup macaroni letters, optional (*W) | 60 mL |
| ¼ cup lentils | 60 mL | | |
| ¼ cup pot barley | 60 mL | 2 cups tomato juice (*F) | 500 mL |
| 2 onions, chopped | | | |
| 4 celery stalks, chopped | | Salt, pepper to taste | |
| 1 large potato, chopped | | 1 teaspoon Worcestershire sauce | 5 mL |

Rinse off bones quickly in cold water and trim off fat. Place in large kettle or soup pot and cover with cold water. Bring to a boil and simmer for an hour. Skim off fat and scum.

Place split peas, lentils and barley in a bowl. Cover with boiling water and let soak for an hour while the bones are cooking. Drain soaked vegetables and add to pot. Simmer for another hour.

Add onions, celery, potato, carrots, macaroni, juice, salt and pepper to taste and Worcestershire sauce. Simmer another hour, stirring now and then. Remove bones. If desired meat can be removed from bones and returned to soup.

Soup will taste even better when served the next day.

# Basic Soup

Put everything you can into it.

| | | | | |
|---|---|---|---|---|
| ½ gallon water | 3 L | | 1 cup of celery, chopped | 250 mL |
| 3 pounds soup bones | 1.3 K | | 1 cup carrots, chopped | 250 mL |
| 1 large onion | | | ¼ cup rice | 60 mL |
| 1 28-ounce can tomatoes | 796 mL | | | |
| 2 teaspoons salt | 10 mL | | | |

Place the water, soup bones, onion, tomatoes and salt in a large pot. Cover and simmer for 2–3 hours. Add celery, carrots and rice. Simmer for another 30 minutes.

Free of: E W G S

Can be free of: M C F

# Potato Soup

| | | | | |
|---|---|---|---|---|
| 5 cups sliced raw potatoes | 1250 mL | | 1 tablespoon butter or milk-free margarine (*C, F) | 15 mL |
| 1 stalk celery, finely chopped | | | Milk, water or stock as needed (*M) | |
| 1 tablespoon minced onion | 15 mL | | Salt and pepper to taste | |
| 1 medium carrot, grated | | | | |

Barely cover vegetables with water and simmer until well cooked, about 10 minutes. Mash in own liquid and add butter and enough milk to give desired consistency. Season. Reheat and serve.

## Variation
1 cup (250 mL) frozen corn or suitable brand creamed corn can be substituted for carrots.

**Free of: E C**

**Can be free of: W G S**

**Contains: M F**

# Tomato Bisque

| | | | | |
|---|---|---|---|---|
| 1 | 28-ounce can tomatoes | 796 mL | 1 teaspoon sugar (*S) | 5 mL |
| ½ | onion, sliced | | Salt to taste | |
| 1 | bay leaf | | ¼ teaspoon nutmeg | 1 mL |
| 2 | cups milk | 500 mL | or sweet basil | |
| 1 | beef bouillon cube | | Pepper | |
| | and hot water (*W, G) | | ½ cup dry (suitable) | 125 mL |
| | (or broth equivalent) | | breadcrumbs (*W, G) | |
| | | | 2 tablespoons butter | 25 mL |

Combine tomatoes, onion and bay leaf. Simmer for 10 minutes and press through sieve, or remove bayleaf and put through blender. Slowly stir in milk, and add bouillon cube dissolved in small amount of hot water or broth. Add seasonings. Stir while heating. Do *not* boil. Add crumbs and butter.

**Free of: E W G C S**

**Contains: M F**

# Pizza Spread

| | | | | |
|---|---|---|---|---|
| ½ | pound Cheddar cheese | 250 g | 1 small onion | |
| ½ | pound bacon | 250 g | ¼ teaspoon garlic powder | 1 mL |
| 1 | 10-ounce tin mushrooms, drained | 280 g | 1 teaspoon oregano | 5 mL |
| 1 | small green pepper | | Dash of pepper | |
| | | | 1 7½-ounce tin tomato sauce | 213 g |

Dice or grate cheese. Dice bacon, mushrooms, pepper and onion. If desired, all may be put through food chopper together.

Combine cheese, bacon, vegetables and spices with tomato sauce to moisten. Spread thinly on allowed bread, buns, or crackers. Place on baking sheet in oven at 350°F (180°C) for 10–15 minutes, or until cheese is bubbly and bacon is cooked. This recipe can be prepared in advance and refrigerated.

## Variations
Omit bacon and/or mushrooms from spread. Decorate pizza with crisp bacon strips, sliced mushrooms, salami, pepperoni, or other meat suitable to diet. Use your imagination—every pizza can be different!

## Variation: Mini Pizzas

Free of: M E W G C S

Contains: F

Spoon tomato sauce on top of one large rice cake. Add oregano or other spices, meat (beef, salami), if allowed, green pepper slices, mushrooms or any other allowed topping. Broil for 3 minutes just to heat.

# MAIN DISHES

Dinner is the least difficult meal of the day since meat and vegetables are allowed in most allergy diets. But even these dull after a while. Our section suggests casseroles, unusual meat dishes and sauces, and various vegetable dishes for a change of pace. We hope these recipes will illustrate how to alter traditional dinner recipes into allergy-free ones.

Free of: M E W

Can be free of: G F

Contains: C S

## Polynesian Pork

Serves 4

4 pork chops

1 14-ounce can pine-   398 g
  apple chunks, reserve
  juice

1 tablespoon brown   15 mL
  sugar

1 tablespoon soy   15 mL
  sauce (*G)

1 teaspoon ginger   5 mL

2 tablespoons   25 mL
  cornstarch

2 tablespoons cold   25 mL
  water

1 green pepper,
  chopped (*F)

Brown pork chops in hot frypan. Combine syrup from pineapple, sugar, soy sauce, and ginger. Pour over chops. Cover and simmer for 45 minutes.

Mix cornstarch with water and use to thicken sauce. Add pineapple chunks and green pepper. Cook 5 minutes more. Serve over rice.

*G — Use gluten-free soy sauce or substitute one finely chopped celery stick.

# Sweet and Sour Meat Balls

| | |
|---|---|
| 1 pound ground beef | 500 g |
| ¾ cup finely diced celery | 175 mL |
| ½ cup finely chopped almonds (*F) or substitute | 125 mL |
| 1 teaspoon salt | 5 mL |
| 2 tablespoons minced onion | 25 mL |
| 2 eggs slightly beaten | |
| Cornstarch | |
| Cooking oil | |
| Hot rice | |

### Sauce

| | |
|---|---|
| ½ cup sugar | 125 mL |
| 3 tablespoons cornstarch | 40 mL |
| 1 cup boiling water | 250 mL |
| 2 chicken bouillon cubes (*F, G) | |
| ½ cup vinegar | 125 mL |
| 2 teaspoons soy sauce (*G) | 10 mL |
| ½ cup pineapple juice | 125 mL |
| 1 green pepper, cut in thin strips and lightly sautéed | |
| 1 cup pineapple chunks | 250 mL |

Mix together the first 6 ingredients, and shape into small meat balls less than one inch in diameter. Roll them in cornstarch. Brown slowly in hot oil, cooking about 15 minutes. Turn frequently.

Prepare sauce by mixing sugar and cornstarch in a saucepan. Dissolve bouillon cubes in boiling water and stir into sugar-cornstarch mixture along with vinegar, soy sauce and pineapple juice. Stir-cook until sauce is smooth and slightly thickened. Add green pepper and pineapple pieces. Heat to serving temperature. Pour over meat balls. Serve on hot rice.

The meat balls and sauce may be frozen, if desired.

| Free of: E W G C S |
| :--- |
| Can be free of: M |
| Contains: F |

# Beef Casserole

Serves 6

| | | | | |
| :--- | ---: | :--- | ---: |
| 1½ pounds ground beef | 750 g | 1 teaspoon Worcestershire sauce | 5 mL |
| ¾ pound sliced mushrooms (or 1 10-ounce can) | 350 g 284 g | ½ teaspoon salt Pinch thyme | 2 mL |
| 1 green pepper, chopped | | 6 ounces fine noodles (use rice vermicelli for gluten-free diets) | 170 g |
| 1 cup celery, chopped | 250 mL | | |
| 1 28-ounce can tomatoes | 796 mL | Grated cheese (*M) (omit for milk-free diets) | |
| 1 package dried onion soup mix or chopped onions | | | |

Sauté together beef, mushrooms, pepper and celery. Add tomatoes, soup mix, Worcestershire sauce, salt and thyme. Cook until excess moisture has gone. Cook rice vermicelli or noodles, drain well and add to meat mixture. Place in casserole, adding grated cheese if allowed. Heat in 350° (180°C) oven for ½–¾ hour.

If desired, omit mushrooms, celery and tomatoes and substitute stuffed olives, canned corn niblets and your favorite soup.

| Free of: E W G C S |
| :--- |
| Can be free of: M |
| Contains: F |

# Jambalaya

| | | | | |
| :--- | ---: | :--- | ---: |
| 2 slices chopped bacon | | ¾ cup uncooked rice | 175 mL |
| 2 tablespoons chopped onion | 25 mL | 2 cups cooked ham, chicken or turkey, diced | 500 mL |
| 2 cups tomatoes | 500 mL | Grated Parmesan or Cheddar cheese (*M) (omit for milk-free diet) | |
| 1 cup water | 250 mL | | |
| ½ teaspoon salt | 2 mL | | |
| ¼ teaspoon pepper | 1 mL | | |

Cook bacon slowly, add onion and cook until clear. Add tomatoes, water and seasonings. Bring to boil. Add rice to boiling liquid; lightly stir with fork until mixture comes to boil. Cover tightly, reduce heat and let simmer 20 minutes. When rice is tender and dry, add diced meat. Heat to serving temperature. Add cheese if allowed.

Free of: M E W S

Can be free of: G C

Contains: F

# Hunter's Pepper Steak

Serves 4

| | | | |
|---|---|---|---|
| 1 pound round or sirloin steak, sliced 1/4 inch thick (.5 cm) and cut in serving pieces | 500 g | 1 large green pepper, thinly sliced in rings | |
| 2 tablespoons oil | 25 mL | 2 tablespoons cornstarch (*C) | 25 mL |
| 1 clove garlic, halved | | *or* | |
| 1/4 cup diced onions | 50 mL | 3 tablespoons arrowroot starch | 40 mL |
| 1 teaspoon salt | 5 mL | 1/4 cup cold water | 50 mL |
| Dash pepper | | 2 tablespoons soy sauce (*G) (or fresh ginger and a dash of Worcestershire sauce) | 25 mL |
| 1 beef bouillon cube (*G), dissolved in 1 cup hot water *or* equivalent broth | 250 mL | | |
| 2 cups canned tomatoes | 500 mL | | |

Brown meat slowly in oil (about 15 minutes); add onion and garlic during the last 5 minutes. Add salt, pepper, and bouillon cube dissolved in the hot water. Cover; simmer until meat is almost tender (20–35 minutes, depending on meat). Add tomatoes and green pepper; cook 10 minutes longer. Combine cornstarch, cold water and soy sauce and stir into meat mixture. Bring to boil and cook, stirring constantly for 5 minutes. Remove garlic and discard. Serve meat mixture over rice.

| Free of: M E W G |
|---|
| Contains: F S C |

# Lamb Provençal

Serves 4–6

| | | | | |
|---|---|---|---|---|
| ½ | pound fresh mushrooms *or* | 250 g | ¼ cup brown sugar | 60 mL |
| 1 | 10-ounce can | 284 g | 1 tablespoon cornstarch | 15 mL |
| 1 | onion chopped | | 1 tablespoon Worcestershire sauce | 15 mL |
| 1 | pound ground lamb (or hamburger) | 500 g | ¼ teaspoon ginger | 1 mL |
| 2 | cups tomato juice | 500 mL | 1 bouillon cube (optional) | |

Fry mushrooms, onion and meat together. Add tomato juice, brown sugar, cornstarch, Worcestershire sauce, ginger and bouillon. Cook until thickened.

Serve over rice or mound rice and ring with Lamb Provençal. Garnish with tomato slices and lightly steamed spinach leaves.

| Free of: M E W G S |
|---|
| Can be free of: F |
| Contains: C |

# Basic Wok Recipe

| | | | |
|---|---|---|---|
| 1 pound pork chops or leftover meats | 500 g | 2 cups assorted vegetables, chopped | 500 mL |
| 2 tablespoons oil | 25 mL | ¾ cup allowable broth | 175 mL |
| 1 clove garlic, minced (optional) | | 2 tablespoons soy sauce or sherry | 25 mL |
| 1 teaspoon minced ginger | 5 mL | ¼ teaspoon pepper | 1 mL |
| 6 celery stalks, chopped | | 2 cups bean sprouts | 500 mL |
| 1 green pepper, chopped (*F) | | 2 teaspoons cornstarch | 10 mL |
| 4–5 green onions or 2 cooking onions, chopped | | 2 tablespoons water | 30 mL |

Have all ingredients ready before you begin. Remove fat and bone from meat. Slice across grain into thin strips. Heat oil. Stir in garlic and ginger for 30 seconds. Add pork, stir fry 3–4 minutes. Add celery, vegetables, green pepper, onions, and stir fry 3–4 minutes. Add bean sprouts, stir fry an additional 3 minutes. Add broth, soy sauce and pepper. Reduce heat. Simmer, covered. Combine cornstarch and water. Pour in slowly, stirring constantly until sauce is clear and slightly thickened. Serve over rice.

### Variation
Use any kind of meat, and any combination of vegetables.

Free of: S C

Can be free of: M E W G F

## *Meat Loaf*

| | | | | |
|---|---|---|---|---|
| ½ cup ketchup or juice | 125 mL | 2 teaspoons Worcestershire sauce or soy sauce | 10 mL |
| ½ cup crumbs or crackers (*W, G) (as allowed) cooked rice, tapioca | 125 mL | 2 teaspoons salt | 10 mL |
| | | ½ teaspoon pepper | 2 mL |
| | | 1 egg | |
| 2 tablespoons onion | 30 mL | ¼ cup milk | 50 mL |
| 2 tablespoons green pepper (*F) | 30 mL | 2 pounds meat (mix of beef, pork, veal is nicest) | 1 Kg |
| 2 teaspoons dry mustard | 10 mL | 2 slices bacon (optional) | |

Combine all non-meat ingredients; blend well. Add meat and blend well. Turn into a loaf pan. Top with bacon. Bake at 350°F (180°C) for 1 hour.

Any 2 or 3 of the non-meat ingredients can be omitted depending on diet restrictions without affecting the meat loaf. Elimination of the egg and crumbs will make the product more crumbly, but it will not impair the taste.

| Free of: E W G C S |
| :--- |
| Can be free of: M F |

# Rice and Chicken Casserole

Serves 4

| | | | |
| :--- | :--- | :--- | :--- |
| 2 tablespoons allowed fat | 25 mL | 1 teaspoon salt | 5 mL |
| | | Pepper | |
| ½ cup mushrooms, sliced | 125 mL | 1½ cups diced cooked chicken | 325 mL |
| ¼ cup chopped onion | 50 mL | ¼ teaspoon Worcestershire sauce | 1 mL |
| 1 cup minute rice | 250 mL | ½ cup grated cheese (optional) (*M, F) | 125 mL |
| 2 cups chicken broth | 500 mL | | |

Melt fat in skillet and sauté mushrooms and onion. Add minute rice, chicken broth, salt and pepper. Mix until rice is moistened. Cover and simmer gently for 10 minutes, fluffing rice occasionally. Add chicken, Worcestershire sauce and top with grated cheese. Cook at 350°F (180°C) for 30 minutes.

| Free of: M E W G C S F |
| :--- |

# Spaghetti Squash

Medium-sized squash makes 5–6 average servings.

## To Microwave

Wash squash. With a paring knife or fork, stab the skin a number of times on all sides of the squash. (This step is important to prevent the squash blowing up in a microwave oven.) Put squash in microwave on a paper towel, if you wish; microwave on high heat 15 to 17 minutes until soft. Let squash rest either covered in foil or in microwave oven for 10 minutes. Cut squash in half. Remove centre pulp and seeds. The flesh of the squash separates into strings. With a fork, carefully lift spaghetti strings. Serve with spaghetti sauce.

Squash may be cooked in advance and spaghetti placed in a bowl for reheating in microwave at time of serving.

## To Boil

Boil the squash whole (although larger squash may be cut in half for cooking), remove center pulp and seeds and extract the strands gently with a fork and serve with a spaghetti sauce.

## Variation

Wash squash. Cut in half, remove seeds. Prepare ground meat, onion, celery, green pepper, sauce to moisten, as desired. Fill cavity of squash with meat mix. Place in suitable pan. Bake at 350°F (180°C) until meat is cooked and squash is tender.

Note: Squash is an excellent "filler" food for allergic people. The methods used in this recipe may be adapted to other varieties of squash.

Free of: W G C S

Can be free of: F

Contains: M E

# Bacon and Red Pepper Spaghetti Sauce

Serves 4

8 slices bacon, diced
1 tablespoon olive oil    15 mL
1 tiny red hot pepper
½ teaspoon oregano    2 mL
  (optional)
2 eggs

½ cup grated cheese    125 mL
  Salt and pepper to taste
4 tablespoons melted    60 mL
  butter (*F)
  Rice vermicelli, spaghetti

Fry bacon with oil, whole red pepper and oregano until bacon is brown. Remove pepper pod. Place large serving bowl over hot (not boiling) water. Beat eggs in this bowl until foamy. Add cheese, salt and pepper. Mix well, then stir in butter, bacon and oil. Add well-drained rice vermicelli (or spaghetti if not on gluten and wheat-free diet) to bacon mixture. Toss well and serve with additional grated cheese.

| | | | |
|---|---|---|---|
| Free of: M E W G C S | | | |
| Contains: F | | | |

# Wine Spaghetti Sauce

| | | | |
|---|---|---|---|
| 1 pound ground beef | 500 g | ¼–½ cup dry wine | 50–125 mL |
| Celery | | ¼ teaspoon thyme | 1 mL |
| Green pepper | | 1 tablespoon paprika | 15 mL |
| Zucchini squash | | | |
| Water | | | |

Place a little salt in fry pan and fry ground beef—no oil is necessary. Drain fat. Add chopped vegetables. (The amount may be adjusted to your preference.) Add enough water to cover, then wine, thyme and paprika. Simmer an hour. Add more water if necessary. Thicken if desired with suitable flour.

| | |
|---|---|
| Free of: M E W G S | |
| Can be free of: C F | |

# Tomato-less Spaghetti Sauce

| | | | |
|---|---|---|---|
| ¼ cup milk-free margarine (*C, F) | 50 mL | 2 cups mushrooms, thinly sliced | 500 mL |
| ¼ cup oil (*C) | 60 mL | Salt and pepper | |
| 1 garlic clove, minced | | ¼ teaspoon oregano | 1 mL |

Melt oil and margarine in frying pan; add garlic and mushrooms. Fry until tender, stirring often. Add spices. Pour over hot rice or spaghetti immediately.

### Variation
Substitute shrimp for mushrooms.

# Casserole Potatoes

Free of: M E W G S

Can be free of: C F

4 medium potatoes,
  sliced
1 teaspoon salt       5 mL
1 tablespoon chopped   15 mL
  parsley or parsley flakes

1 cup boiling water    250 mL
2 tablespoons milk-     25 mL
  free margarine (*C, F)

Mix all ingredients in casserole, cover and bake at 375°F (190°C) for one hour.

## Variation
Add onions, spices, vegetables, nuts, seeds.

# Spicy Mashed Potatoes

Free of: M E W G S

Can be free of: C F

2 cups mashed     500 mL
  potatoes, seasoned
  (do not add milk)
2 slices bacon, diced
  and cooked
1 tablespoon chopped   15 mL
  parsley

2 tablespoons      25 mL
  chopped onion
2 tablespoons milk-     25 mL
  free margarine (*C, F)

Combine all ingredients and serve at once.

| Free of: M E W G C S F |
| --- |

# Roasted Potatoes

Carve tiny holes in the sides of raw potatoes and insert baby green onions. Add to roasting pan and cook with roast. Different and delicious.

| Free of: M E W G S |
| --- |
| Can be free of: C F |

# *Herb Rice*

Serves 4–6

| | | | | |
| --- | --- | --- | --- | --- |
| 1 cup uncooked rice | 250 mL | 1 teaspoon salt | 5 mL |
| 2 cups chicken stock, or 2 cups water and 2 chicken cubes | 500 mL | ½ teaspoon rosemary | 2 mL |
| | | ½ teaspoon marjoram | 2 mL |
| 1 tablespoon milk-free margarine (*C, F) | 15 mL | ½ teaspoon thyme | 2 mL |

Combine all ingredients in a pot and bring to a boil. Cover and simmer for 15 minutes. Allow to stand with cover removed for 5 minutes before serving.

# SAUCES, DRESSINGS AND RELISHES

What would a turkey be without the stuffing? Or a hamburger without the fixings? Or a salad without a dressing?

It's the little extras in cooking that make a meal special, and interesting touches are often difficult to obtain on a limited diet. The recipes in this section include down-to-earth suggestions so that even if you cannot use the commercial preparations, you can replace them with your own safe creations.

Free of: M E W G C

Contains: S F

## Tomato Sauce

| | | | |
|---|---|---|---|
| 2½ cups canned tomatoes | 625 mL | 2 tablespoons ketchup | 25 mL |
| 2 stalks celery, diced | | 1 tablespoon brown sugar | 15 mL |
| 1 small onion, diced | | | |
| 1 cup green pepper chopped (optional) | 250 mL | 1 tablespoon vinegar | 15 mL |

Add celery, onion and green pepper to tomatoes and simmer 10 minutes. Add ketchup, sugar and vinegar. Simmer until vegetables are cooked. This may be thickened with a gluten-free flour, if desired.

Free of: M E W G C F

Contains: S

## Soy Sauce

Soy sauce contains gluten and wheat. Ingredients include protein extracts from corn and soy beans, wheat, parts of corn and cane, water, and salt.

If anyone wants to experiment with a homemade soy sauce the ingredients are: salt, hot water, molasses or caramel.

The flavor changes with the heat of the water; experiment until you find the right combination of ingredients. It won't be real soy sauce but it makes a good substitute. This should be used in our recipes calling for soy sauce that are marked wheat and gluten free.

## Variation

Soy sauce substitute can be made by taking 2 beef bouillon cubes and dissolving them in boiling water—⅛ cup (25 mL) or less. The more concentrated the tastier it is. Use on chow mein or other Chinese-style dishes. Good!

Free of: M E W G S

Can be free of: C F

# White Sauce #1

| | | | |
|---|---|---|---|
| 1 tablespoon milk-free margarine (*C, F) | 15 mL | ¼ teaspoon salt | 1 mL |
| 1½ teaspoons potato starch or any other gluten-free starch | 7 mL | ½ cup soybean milk | 125 mL |
| | | 1 teaspoon dried parsley (optional) | 5 mL |

Melt margarine in saucepan. Add starch and salt and stir until well mixed. Add milk and parsley and continue stirring until mixture thickens.

Free of: M E S

Can be free of: C F

Contains: W G

# White Sauce #2

| | | | |
|---|---|---|---|
| 1 tablespoon milk-free margarine (*C, F) | 15 mL | 1½ tablespoons flour | 25 mL |
| 1 cup cold water or stock | 250 mL | | |

Place margarine in a pan and melt. Shake water and flour together in a tightly capped jar. Pour into pan with melted margarine. Cook and stir until thickened.

Free of: E W G C S

Can be free of: F

Contains: M

# White Sauce #3

| | | | |
|---|---|---|---|
| 1 tablespoon butter (*F) | 15 mL | 1 cup milk | 250 mL |
| 1 tablespoon potato flour | 15 mL | Salt to taste | |

Melt butter and add potato flour, stirring until blended. To butter-flour mixture, slowly add the milk, stirring constantly until well blended.

If a thicker sauce is desired, increase butter and potato flour to 2 tablespoons (30 mL) each.

# Beef Broth

This stock can be used in place of a beef bouillon cube.

Simmer beef bones, fresh meat 3–4 hours, cooked meat (from roast) for 1–2 hours in water to cover. A bay leaf, salt and vegetable scraps, if desired, add to flavor. Remove scum while simmering. Strain soup, chill, remove fat (store in a tightly covered jar). Broth is ready for use.

It will keep for several days. It may then be brought to a boil, cooled and returned to the tightly covered jar and kept for several days longer. Poultry and vegetable broth can be similarly made.

Free of: M E W G

Can be free of: C S

Contains: F

# Sauce Piquant

| | | | | |
|---|---|---|---|---|
| 3 tablespoons white wine or vegetable juice | 40 mL | 1 cup beef broth | 250 mL |
| 1½ tablespoons vinegar | 22 mL | 1½ tablespoons pickle relish (*S) and/or parsley | 22 mL |
| 1 teaspoon onion, chopped | 5 mL | 1 tablespoon corn-starch (*C) (optional) | 15 mL |

Cook together wine, vinegar and onion for 5 minutes. Stir in beef broth or juice and bring to a boil. Add pickle relish and parsley. Serve with any meat. Thicken with cornstarch, if desired.

Free of: M E W G

Contains: C S F

# Sweet and Sour Sauce

Makes 4–5 servings

| | | | |
|---|---|---|---|
| 1 cup sugar | 250 mL | ½ cup vinegar | 125 mL |
| 3 tablespoons corn-starch | 40 mL | 1 19-ounce can pineapple tid-bits (separated) | 540 mL |
| Pinch of garlic powder | | | |
| 1½ cups tomato juice | 375 mL | | |

In a saucepan mix sugar, cornstarch and garlic powder. Stir in tomato juice, pineapple juice and vinegar while heating. Bring to boil, stirring until thickened. Add the pineapple tid-bits. Heat thoroughly.

# *Tartar Sauce*

| | | | |
|---|---|---|---|
| 1 cup mayonnaise (*C, E, W, G, S) (as allowed) | 250 mL | 1 slice finely chopped onion | |
| 4 tablespoons fresh lemon juice | 50 mL | ⅛ cup minced parsley | 25 mL |
| ½ cup finely diced cucumber (F) | 125 mL | | |

Mix all ingredients together. Let stand overnight for best flavor. Serve chilled.

# *Ginger Sauce*

| | | | |
|---|---|---|---|
| 1 cup water | 250 mL | ⅓ cup chopped mushrooms | 75 mL |
| ¼ cup sugar | 60 mL | ½ cup chopped onion | 125 mL |
| 1 tablespoon soy sauce (*G, F) | 15 mL | Salt to taste | |
| ¼ cup vinegar | 60 mL | 2 tablespoons cornstarch | 25 mL |
| 3 tablespoons chopped candied ginger | 40 mL | | |

Combine water, sugar, soy sauce, vinegar and candied ginger in a saucepan and bring to a boil. Add mushrooms, onion and salt. Cook about 10 minutes. Stir in cornstarch mixed with a little water. Heat until slightly thickened and no raw starch taste remains. Serve over fish or chicken.

| Free of: E W G |
| --- |
| Can be free of: C S F |
| Contains: M |

# Eggless Mayonnaise

Makes 1 cup

| | | | |
| --- | --- | --- | --- |
| ½ teaspoon salt | 2 mL | 2 tablespoons ice water | 25 mL |
| ½ teaspoon dry mustard | 2 mL | ¾ cup salad oil (*C, F) | 175 mL |
| ¼ teaspoon paprika | 1 mL | 3 tablespoons lemon juice | 40 mL |
| 1 teaspoon granulated sugar (optional) (*S) | 5 mL | | |
| Dash cayenne pepper | | *or* 2 tablespoons wine vinegar | 25 mL |
| ¼ cup powdered skim milk | 60 mL | | |

Place deep, medium-sized bowl and electric mixer beaters in refrigerator until thoroughly chilled.

In chilled bowl, mix together salt, mustard, paprika, sugar, pepper, powdered milk and water.

With mixer at highest speed add 2 tablespoons (25 mL) oil, drop by drop. Continue to add oil, by half teaspoonfuls, with beater on, until 2 more tablespoons (25 mL) have been added. With continuous beating, add remaining oil by the teaspoonful. Slowly beat in lemon juice or vinegar. Continue to beat until mayonnaise is thick and smooth. Store in warmest part of refrigerator.

## Variation

For delicious Russian dressing, beat ¼ cup (60 mL) chili sauce into 1 cup (250 mL) eggless mayonnaise. If you wish an even sharper flavor, add, in addition to the chili sauce, 1 tablespoon (15 mL) each finely minced onion and green pepper.

# Potato Flour Mayonnaise

Free of: M E W G

Can be free of: S C F

| | | | | |
|---|---|---|---|---|
| 1½ | tablespoons potato flour | 20 mL | ¾ | cup boiling water | 175 mL |

1½ tablespoons potato flour — 20 mL

¼ teaspoon dry mustard — 1 mL

½ teaspoon salt — 2 mL

2 teaspoons sugar (*S) — 10 mL

¼ cup cold water — 60 mL

¾ cup boiling water — 175 mL

2 tablespoons lemon juice — 25 mL

1 tablespoon white vinegar — 15 mL

½ cup vegetable oil (*C, F) — 125 mL

Salt and pepper

Mix dry ingredients in saucepan, then stir in cold water and mix well. Add hot water and cook just till mixture is clear. Cool to lukewarm, then gradually add remaining ingredients, beating constantly.

Free of: M E W G C S

Contains: F

# French Dressing

4 tablespoons lemon juice — 60 mL

2 tablespoons powdered pectin — 30 mL

½ cup water — 125 mL

¼ teaspoon paprika — 1 mL

1 tablespoon tomato paste — 15 mL

Combine all ingredients, mix well and chill. Makes ¾ cup (175 mL).

# Rice Stuffing

Free of: M E W G S

Can be free of: C F

Stuffs 1 6-pound (2.75 Kg) chicken

| | | | |
|---|---|---|---|
| 1 tablespoon milk-free margarine (*C, F) | 15 mL | 2 cups cooked rice | 1000 mL |
| ½ cup finely chopped onion | 125 mL | ¾ teaspoon salt | 3 mL |
| ½ cup finely chopped celery | 125 mL | ¼ teaspoon each marjoram, sage, savory, thyme | 1 mL |
| ¼ cup finely chopped green pepper | 60 mL | Pinch of pepper | |
| 1 chicken liver and heart finely chopped | | ¼ cup chopped pecans, soy nuts, or sunflower seeds | 60 mL |
| | | ¼ cup chopped celery leaves | 60 mL |

Melt margarine in frying pan and sauté onion, celery, green pepper, liver and heart. Mix in rest of ingredients. Stuff chicken loosely.

**Note:** If allowed, one small beaten egg can be added at end of mixing.

Free of: M E W G

Can be free of: C S

Contains: F

# Orange Rice Stuffing

| | | | |
|---|---|---|---|
| ¼ cup milk-free margarine (*C, F) | 60 mL | ½ teaspoon salt | 2 mL |
| 2 tablespoons minced onion | 25 mL | ½ teaspoon sugar (*S) | 2 mL |
| ⅔ cup orange juice (F) | 150 mL | ½ teaspoon poultry seasoning | 2 mL |
| ½ cup chopped celery | 125 mL | ⅔ cup cooked rice | 150 mL |

Fry onion in margarine. Add next five ingredients. Mix and bring to boil. Add rice, mix until completely moistened, cover tightly, remove from heat and let stand for 5 minutes. Uncover and fluff with fork. Stuff bird loosely.

# Meat and Poultry Stuffing

Makes 3 cups or 700 mL

**Free of: E W S**

**Can be free of: M C F**

**Contains: G**

| | |
|---|---|
| 24 rye crackers | |
| ¾ cup hot meat stock | 175 mL |
| ¼ cup butter or milk-free margarine (*M, C, F) | 60 mL |
| ¼ cup finely cut celery | 60 mL |
| 2 tablespoons finely cut parsley | 25 mL |
| 2 tablespoons finely cut green pepper | 25 mL |
| 2 tablespoons finely cut onion | 25 mL |
| ½ teaspoon poultry seasoning | 2 mL |
| ¼ teaspoon salt | 1 mL |
| ⅛ teaspoon pepper | .5 mL |

Break crackers into small pieces. Soak in hot stock. Add remaining ingredients. Mix well. Stuff bird or place in greased casserole and bake for 30 minutes, until brown, at 325°F (160°C).

**Free of: M E W G C S F**

# Rhubarb Ketchup

| | |
|---|---|
| 4 cups fresh or frozen rhubarb | 1000 mL |
| 1 cup water | 250 mL |
| ¼ cup chopped onion | 60 mL |
| ½ cup honey | 125 mL |
| ¼ cup white vinegar | 60 mL |
| ½ teaspoon salt | 2 mL |
| ¼–½ teaspoon cinnamon | 1–2 mL |

Combine rhubarb, water, onion, honey and vinegar in a large saucepan. Boil slowly until thick, stirring frequently. Add salt and cinnamon and cook 5 minutes more. Cool. Place in blender until a ketchup-like consistency is reached. Refrigerate in a covered container.

Free of: M E W G C F

Contains: S

# Dill Green Beans

| | | | | |
|---|---|---|---|---|
| 3 pounds green beans | 1.5 Kg | 4 tablespoons sugar | 50 mL |
| 2 cups water | 500 mL | 1 dash cayenne pepper | |
| 2 cups white vinegar | 500 mL | 1 teaspoon dill per pint | 5 mL |
| 4 tablespoons salt | 50 mL | 2 garlic cloves per pint | |

Boil beans 2–5 minutes to blanch. Cool in ice water. Make brine of water, vinegar, salt, sugar, and cayenne, and bring to boil. Pack beans in sterilized pint sealers. Add dill and garlic. Pour boiling liquid over beans and seal at once.

Free of: M E W G C F

Contains: S

# Curried Zucchini Relish

| | | | |
|---|---|---|---|
| 16 medium-sized ripe zucchini, about 4 pounds | 2 Kg | 2 large cloves garlic, crushed | |
| 6 medium-sized onions finely chopped | | 1 tablespoon curry powder | 15 mL |
| 6 stalks celery | | 1½ teaspoons each of celery seed and mustard seed | 7 mL |
| ½ cup coarse salt | 125 mL | 1 red pepper, chopped (optional) | |
| 3½ cups white vinegar | 875 mL | | |
| 2¾ cups granulated sugar | 675 mL | | |

Scrub zucchini, trim, but do not peel. Finely chop using a sharp knife or julienne in a food processor. Measure out 12 cups (3 litres) and combine in a large bowl with onions and celery. Stir in salt until evenly distributed. Weigh down with a plate and leave at room temperature for 2–4 hours. Then drain and rinse well with cold water to remove salt.

Combine vinegar, sugar, garlic and seasoning in a large heavy-bottomed saucepan. Bring to a boil gently, and simmer, covered, for 20 minutes. Add the drained vegetable mixture and red pepper. Bring to a boil again. Reduce heat and simmer, covered for 10 minutes. Continue simmering while packing one hot sterilized jar at a time. Leave one inch of water at top of each jar. Make sure zucchini is well covered with liquid. Adjust lids on jars as soon as they are filled and tightly seal them. Place jars in a large kettle of boiling water—5 minutes for pint jars and 10 minutes for quart ones.

Free of: M E W G S

Can be free of: C F

# *Wild Rice Casserole or Stove-top Stuffing*

Serves 4 as casserole
or stuffs one large bird

| | | |
|---|---|---|
| 1 cup wild rice | 250 mL | |
| 1 tablespoon oil (*C, F) | 15 mL | |
| 1 tablespoon minced onion | 15 mL | |
| 1 teaspoon salt | 5 mL | |
| 2½ cups water or chicken broth | 625 mL | |

*May add if desired*

| | |
|---|---|
| 2 cups chopped mushrooms | 500 mL |
| ½ cup celery | 125 mL |
| ½ teaspoon marjoram | 2 mL |
| ½ teaspoon thyme | 2 mL |

Wash rice thoroughly. Sauté onion in oil until tender. Add rice, salt, liquid, bring to boil. Stir once; reduce heat. Cover tightly and cook over low heat about 45 minutes, until liquid is absorbed. Add other ingredients as desired. Transfer to oiled shallow baking dish and place in slow oven 325°F (160°C) for 10–15 minutes or until rice grains are separate and dry.

# BREADS

Since bread is such a common part of our diet we feel at a loss when wheat and/or yeast is removed. Breads without wheat flour are very difficult to make. Expect a few bricks, a few soups and a few messes. But don't give up. Work on improving your techniques until you get one that works. Once you do, make it several times exactly as the recipe shows and then experiment.

Two of the most important things to look at during the brick stage are the place the dough rises and the oven temperature. The ideal temperature for raising bread is 90°F (32°C). If the place is too cold, the raising takes too long; too drafty and the dough will be lopsided; too hot—the yeast is killed or air bubbles form. Since oven temperature is also critical, either have your oven calibrated by a serviceman or purchase an independent oven thermometer.

For those who cannot use yeast, we have included some good yeast-free bread recipes; these will have Y in the "Free of" section of the legend.

Do not limit yourself to the recipes in this section. Look at the breads in the dessert section and prepare these with reduced sugar. A carrot bread or a pear bread is delicious for breakfast or lunch. If you are making a quick bread with rice or corn flour, allow rice or corn-bread mix to rest in mixing bowl without leavening. Mix in required amount of leavening gently just before pouring into pan.

Free of: E W C

Can be free of: F

Contains: M G S Y

## Rye Flour Bread

Y = Yeast

| | | | | |
|---|---|---|---|---|
| 1 cake compressed yeast | | 2 tablespoons butter (*F) | 25 mL |
| ½ cup water 85°F (29°C) | 125 mL | 1 tablespoon sugar | 15 mL |
| | | 2 teaspoons salt | 10 mL |
| 2 cups milk | 500 mL | 6 cups rye flour | 1500 mL |

68

Dissolve yeast in water and let sit for 10 minutes. Scald milk. As it cools add butter, sugar and salt. When it reaches about 85°F (29°C), add the yeast mixture and stir in 2 cups (500 mL) rye flour. Let this rise 40 minutes. Then add slowly, while stirring, 3 cups (750 mL) rye flour. Let rise 40 more minutes. Sprinkle a board with the remaining 1 cup (250 mL) rye flour.

Knead dough for 10 minutes. Divide it into four parts; shape into round or long loaves. Place on a well-greased cookie sheet. Grease top of the loaves and let rise 1 hour. Preheat oven to 350°F (180°C). Bake for 1 hour.

Free of: Y M E S

Can be free of: C F

Contains: W G

# *Bannoch Bread*

Bannoch bread came from Scotland and northern England and was brought to Canada by immigrants. Originally bannoch was made from oat, rye or barley flour with no leavening.

| | | | |
|---|---|---|---|
| 2 cups all-purpose flour | 500 mL | ¼ cup shortening or lard (*C, F) | 60 mL |
| 3 teaspoons baking powder | 15 mL | ¾ cup water | 175 mL |
| 1 teaspoon salt | 5 mL | | |

Sift flour, baking powder and salt. Cut in shortening or lard. Add water and mix quickly. Turn out onto floured board and knead 30 seconds. Pat into 10 inch (25 cm) round (to fit frypan). Cook in lightly greased, heated frypan over medium heat, about 15 minutes a side. This can be tricky to turn, so you can cut circle into 4 wedges first, if you like.

Can be split open for sandwiches or hamburgers.

Free of: M E W

Can be free of: C F

Contains: Y G S

# Banana Rye Bread

Makes 2 loaves

| | | | | |
|---|---|---|---|---|
| 2¼ cups mashed ripe bananas (5–6 bananas) | 550 mL | 1 tablespoon salt | 15 mL |
| | | 1½ tablespoons sugar | 22 mL |
| 2 cakes compressed yeast | | 3 tablespoons melted shortening (*C, F) | 45 mL |
| 3 tablespoons lukewarm water | 45 mL | 5¼–6 cups light rye flour | 1250–1500 mL |

Use fully ripe bananas—the yellow peel should be flecked with brown.

Dissolve yeast in water. Mix together salt, sugar, shortening and bananas. Add half the flour and beat until smooth. Beat in the dissolved yeast. Add remaining flour gradually and mix well.

Turn out dough onto a floured board. Knead about 8 minutes, adding just enough additional rye flour to prevent sticking. Place dough into a lightly greased bowl. Cover and let rise until double in bulk, about 2 hours.

Turn out again onto floured board and knead lightly about 2 minutes. Shape dough into 2 loaves. Place into lightly greased (8 inch × 4 inch × 3 inch) (20 cm × 10 cm × 8 cm) bread pans. Cover and let rise again until double in bulk, about 1 hour.

Bake at 425°F (220°C) for 5–10 minutes, or until crust begins to brown. Reduce temperature to 350°F (180°C) and bake 35–40 minutes longer, or until bread is done. Remove from pans. Brush top crusts with water.

# Biscuit Mix

| | | | |
|---|---|---|---|
| 9 cups all-purpose flour | 2 L | ¼ cup baking powder | 60 mL |
| 2 tablespoons salt | 25 mL | 2 cups shortening (*C, F) | 500 mL |

Sift flour, salt and baking powder together. Mix in shortening in a large bowl until it resembles corn meal. Store in refrigerator. This recipe can be used in various quick breads and biscuits.

# Baking Powder Biscuits

Makes about 18 biscuits

3 cups Biscuit Mix    750 mL
  (see above)
2 tablespoons liquid    25 mL
  shortening (*C, F), plus
  water to make ¾ cup
  (175 mL)

Mix ingredients together lightly. Turn out onto floured board and pat to ½ inch (1 cm) thickness. Cut with 2 inch (5 cm) cookie cutter. Bake at 450°F (230°C) for 15 minutes. Biscuits may be frozen for future use.

Free of: Y E W G S

Can be free of: M F

Contains: C

# Crisp Corn Pone

| | | | |
|---|---|---|---|
| 1 cup corn meal | 250 mL | 2 teaspoons melted | 10 mL |
| ½ teaspoon salt | 2 mL | fat or butter (*M, F) | |
| 1 cup boiling water | 250 mL | | |

Sift cornmeal and salt through coarse sifter. Add boiling water and stir into a stiff dough. Dip hands in cold water. Mould dough into 2 flat thin oval cakes.

Place on well-greased hot griddle or skillet. Brush cakes with melted fat. Bake at 450°F (230°C) for 20 minutes. Break into pieces and serve hot with butter or margarine. Delicious with maple syrup or corn syrup served on top.

Free of: Y W G S

Can be free of: C F

Contains: M E

# Chipa Paraguay

Makes 12 doughnut-shaped rounds

| | | | |
|---|---|---|---|
| 2½ cups potato starch | 625 mL | 1 teaspoon aniseed | 5 mL |
| | | 3 eggs | |
| 2 teaspoons baking powder | 10 mL | 1 cup freshly grated Parmesan *or* old Cheddar cheese (*F) | 250 mL |
| ½ teaspoon salt | 2 mL | | |
| 6 tablespoons butter or margarine (*C, F) | 80 mL | 6 tablespoons milk | 80 mL |

Sift potato starch, baking powder and salt together. In a large bowl, cream margarine until soft, stir in aniseed. Beat in eggs, one at a time, and cheese. Stir in dry ingredients, one third at a time, adding alternately with milk, until dough is partially blended; then knead with hands until completely blended.

Cut dough into 12 even pieces; roll each with hands into a 7 inch (18 cm) long strip, form into a circle, pinching ends to seal. Place an inch (2.5 cm) apart on a large greased cookie sheet. Bake at 375°F (190°C) for 35 minutes or until golden and lightly cracked. Remove from cookie sheet, cool on wire racks.

**Note:** Dough can be made in many different shapes—experiment!

Free of: Y W G

Can be free of: M F

Contains: E S C

# *Everyday Bread*

| | | | |
|---|---|---|---|
| ½ cup allowed cooking oil (*F) | 125 mL | ½ teaspoon salt | 2 mL |
| ⅔ cup sugar | 150 mL | 1 teaspoon cinnamon | 5 mL |
| 3 eggs | | 1¼ cups corn starch | 315 mL |
| 1 cup shredded raw carrots | 250 mL | ¼ cup potato flour | 60 mL |
| 2 teaspoons baking powder | 10 mL | ⅓ cup milk (*M) or juice (*F) | 75 mL |
| 1 teaspoon baking soda | 5 mL | ½ teaspoon lemon extract (Optional) (*F) | 2 mL |

Using mixer, blend oil, sugar and eggs. Measure and stir together dry ingredients. Add dry ingredients and milk/juice alternately to oil-sugar-egg mix. Add lemon extract. Fold in carrots. Work quickly as batter rises quickly.

Pour batter into greased 5½ inch × 9½ inch × 4 inch (14 cm × 24 cm × 10 cm) loaf pan. Bake at 350°F (180°C) for 55–60 minutes or until cake tester comes out clean. Cool 15 minutes and remove from pan. Place on rack to cool completely. Great for sandwiches.

## *Variation*
Substitute ¾ cup finely crushed, drained unsweetened pineapple for carrots and reduce sugar to ½ cup (125 mL).

Free of: Y

Can be free of: G F S C

Contains: M E W

# Gluten-Free Bread

| | | | | |
|---|---|---|---|---|
| 1½ cups + 1 tablespoon wheat starch flour (*G) | 390 mL | | ¼ cup margarine or butter (*C, F) | 50 mL |
| 1 tablespoon sugar (optional) | 15 mL | | 1 cup warm milk | 250 mL |
| Dash of salt | | | 2 egg whites | |

Sift dry ingredients into a bowl, rub in the margarine with pastry blender until it looks mealy. Mix in warm milk to make a batter consistency. Add egg whites (beaten, not too stiff). Mix lightly and pour into greased loaf pan. Bake at 450°F (230°C) for 10 minutes, then reduce temperature to 300°F (150°C) for a further 30 minutes.

Can be free of: G

Contains: M E Y W S F

# Raisin Bread

| | | | | |
|---|---|---|---|---|
| ½ cup raisins | 125 mL | | 1 teaspoon baking powder | 5 mL |
| ¼ cup lukewarm water | 60 mL | | 1 tablespoon sugar | 15 mL |
| ¾ ounce compressed yeast (dissolved by sprinkling over surface of water) | 20 g | | 1 teaspoon salt | 5 mL |
| | | | 1 tablespoon oil | 15 mL |
| | | | 1 egg | |
| 1⅞ cups wheat starch flour (*G) | 475 mL | | ½ cup scalded milk, cooled to lukewarm | 125 mL |
| 5 tablespoons potato flour | 75 mL | | ¼ cup cream-style cottage cheese | 60 mL |
| ⅓ cup skim milk powder | 75 mL | | | |

Dredge raisins in small amount of flour. Dissolve yeast in lukewarm water. Mix flours, skim milk powder and baking powder in large bowl. Mix sugar, salt, oil, egg, milk and cottage cheese. Combine yeast-water mixture with sugar-cheese mixture and add to dry ingredients. Blend in mixer 4 minutes at low speed. Add raisins, mix again.

Let batter rise in warm place about 30–35 minutes until double in bulk. Mix down in mixer again for 4 minutes at low speed. Pour into small greased loaf pan (half full). Sprinkle top with a cinnamon and sugar mixture if desired. Let rise until double its bulk again, until dough reaches top of pan (about 15 minutes). Bake at 400°F (200°C) for 10 minutes, reduce heat to 350°F (180°C) and continue to bake for 25 minutes.

Free of: Y M E W G

Can be free of: C F

Contains: S

# Rice Wafers

| | | | |
|---|---|---|---|
| 3 tablespoons shortening (*C, F) | 50 mL | ½ teaspoon salt | 2 mL |
| 2 tablespoons brown sugar | 25 mL | 3 teaspoons baking powder | 15 mL |
| 1 teaspoon vanilla | 5 mL | 1 cup water, approximately | 250 mL |
| 2 cups rice flour | 500 mL | | |

Cream shortening and sugar. Add vanilla. Sift together rice flour, salt and baking powder. Stir into shortening-sugar mixture, alternately with water, adding just enough water to make a thick dough. Roll thinly on a board dusted with rice flour. Cut into desired shapes and place on greased cookie sheet. Bake at 325°F (160°C) until faintly brown, about 10 minutes.

Free of: Y M E W

Can be free of: C F

Contains: S G

# Rye Potato-Starch Bread

The texture is almost that of a sweet bread—moist and rather crumbly. This bread is good toasted.

| | | | | |
|---|---|---|---|---|
| 3¼ cups rye flour | 800 mL | 1 teaspoon salt | 5 mL |
| ¾ cup potato starch | 175 mL | ¼ cup melted shortening (*C, F) | 60 mL |
| 4 tablespoons baking powder | 60 mL | 2¼ cups water (room temperature) | 550 mL |
| 4 teaspoons sugar | 20 mL | | |

Measure dry ingredients without sifting. Mix together very thoroughly. Mix melted shortening and water together, add to dry ingredients. Mix well. Pour into 2 greased 9 inch × 5 inch (23 cm × 13 cm) loaf pans and bake at 325°F (160°C) for 1¼ hours.

Free of: Y M E W

Can be free of: C F

Contains: G S

# Rye-Rice Bread

| | | | | |
|---|---|---|---|---|
| 1½ cups light rye flour | 375 mL | ½ teaspoon salt | 2 mL |
| ½ cup rice flour | 125 mL | 1¼ cups water | 300 mL |
| 3 tablespoons baking powder | 45 mL | 2 tablespoons melted shortening (*C, F) or oil | 30 mL |
| 2 teaspoons sugar | 10 mL | | |

Mix dry ingredients together well. Add the water and beat for 2 minutes. Add shortening and beat for 1 minute. Bake in well-greased loaf pan at 350°F (180°C) for 10 minutes, reduce oven setting to 300°F (150°C) and bake 1 hour. This bread slices well when cold. If wrapped in plastic and refrigerated it will slice better the second day and be less likely to crumble.

# *Yeast-Free Bread*

| | | | | |
|---|---|---|---|---|
| 4 cups whole-wheat flour | 1000 mL | | 2 tablespoons oil (*C, F) | 30 mL |
| 2 tablespoons baking powder | 30 mL | | 2 cups milk (*M) or water | 500 mL |
| 1 teaspoon salt | 5 mL | | | |
| 2 tablespoons wheat germ | 30 mL | | | |

Mix flour, baking powder, salt and wheat germ. Mix together oil and milk or water. Add to dry ingredients and mix well. Place on floured board and knead 3–4 times. Shape into loaf and put in greased bread tin. Bake at 400°F (200°C) for 10 minutes, then lower oven to 325°F (160°C) and bake 1 hour more.

## *Hamburger and Hot Dog Rolls*

Use your specific diet bread recipe to make non-allergic buns.

For hamburger buns, grease 2½ inch deep (6 cm) aluminum foil baking cups. Put about ½ cup (125 mL) dough in each cup. Bake 15 minutes.

For hot dog buns, make your own baking cups out of heavy aluminum foil. Grease and fill with ½ cup (125 mL) dough. Place cups on cookie sheet and bake 15 minutes.

If the family goes to a restaurant for lunch, take one of these buns along and ask the waiter to just bring you the meat! Some restaurants will even warm your bun and bring it back all made up, along with the other hamburgers. Be sure the meat used contains no allergens.

## Variations on Bread

Use one-quarter of the basic bread mixture that suits your diet and add any one of the following combinations after the second kneading. Be sure the ingredients are well mixed in during the final kneading process. Set to rise and bake as instructed.

| | | |
|---|---|---|
| *Raisin loaf* | ¾ cup floured raisins | 175 mL |
| | 2 tablespoons cinnamon | 25 mL |
| *Herb loaf* | 1 tablespoon dill weed | 15 mL |
| | 1 tablespoon sweet basil | 15 mL |
| | 1 tablespoon parsley flakes | 15 mL |
| | 1 tablespoon oregano | 15 mL |
| *Fruit loaf:* | 1 cup floured chopped fruits, peel, cherries | 250 mL |
| | ½ cup floured raisins | 125 mL |
| | ¼ cup chopped nut meats | 60 mL |

# DESSERTS

One of the things people miss most when they begin allergy diets is sweets. If an old favorite is no longer allowed, try adapting the recipe. If that fails, our wide selection hopefully can supply new delights. This section includes puddings, dessert breads, cookies, ice creams, cakes and other goodies. At first, results might not look right, but will probably taste pretty good. This is where the fun begins. Practise and experiment until the look and taste are pleasing to you. Enjoy yourself!

Free of: E W G C S F

Contains: M

## Chocolate Mousse

Serves 6

| | | | | |
|---|---|---|---|---|
| 1 | tablespoon unflavored gelatin | 15 mL | ½ teaspoon vanilla extract | 2 mL |
| 2 | cups cold milk | 500 mL | Sweetener tablets equal to 6 teaspoons sugar | 30 mL |
| 1 | square unsweetened chocolate | | | |
| ¼ | teaspoon salt | 1 mL | | |

Soften gelatin in ½ cup cold milk. Heat remainder of milk. When hot, add chocolate and continue heating, without letting milk boil, until square has melted.

Add gelatin/cold milk to chocolate milk, and heat until just below boiling point. Remove from heat and mix in salt, vanilla and sweetener. Chill about 1½ hours or until firm.

Beat mixture until it is fluffy, divide among serving dishes and return to refrigerator. Decorate with sweetened whipped cream and/or chocolate shavings.

| Free of: E W G C |
| Contains: M S F |

# Almond Delight

| 1 envelope gelatin | | 1 cup water | 250 mL |
| ¼ cup cold water | 60 mL | 1 cup cold milk | 250 mL |
| ⅓ cup sugar | 75 mL | 1 teaspoon almond extract | 5 mL |

Soak gelatin in cold water until softened. Heat sugar and water to boiling; add gelatin mixture; stir until gelatin has dissolved. Add milk and almond extract. Stir; chill in large bowl until set. Spoon into serving dishes. (This dessert should be *very* delicate; add more water next time if gel doesn't break easily.) Top with drained, chilled fruit cocktail or mandarin orange sections.

| Free of: M E W G S |
| Can be free of: C |
| Contains: F |

# No-Bake Applesauce Crisp

Serves 5

| 2 tablespoons milk-free margarine (*C) | 25 mL | 2 cups applesauce, unsweetened | 500 mL |
| 3 cups corn flakes or rice flakes | 750 mL | | |

Melt margarine. Add cereal and heat until golden brown, stirring constantly. Place alternate layers of applesauce and cereal in shallow serving dish or sherbet glasses, beginning with applesauce and ending with cereal. Applesauce could be heated if a hot dish is preferred. Serve at once. Garnish with cream, topping or ice cream, if allowed.

# Fluff

| | | | |
|---|---|---|---|
| 1 envelope or 3 teaspoons gelatin | 15 mL | 1½ cups milk (fresh, evaporated, powdered or soy) (*M) | 375 mL |
| 3 tablespoons hot water | 50 mL | Flavoring, coloring if allowed (*F) | |
| 2 tablespoons sugar, honey or artificial sweetener (*S) | 30 mL | | |

Dissolve gelatin in hot water. Add sugar and stir gradually into milk. Flavor to taste. Chill. Top with strawberries or other seasonal fruits, or with colored mini-marshmallows.

# Fruit Balls

Makes 25–36 balls, depending on size

| | | | |
|---|---|---|---|
| 2 eggs | | 2 tablespoons flour (*W, G) | 30 mL |
| 1 tablespoon soft butter or milk-free margarine (*M, C, F) | 15 mL | 1 teaspoon baking powder | 5 mL |
| ¾ cup liquid honey | 175 mL | ¼ teaspoon salt | 1 mL |
| ½ teaspoon vanilla | 2 mL | 1 cup chopped dates | 250 mL |
| ½ cup rolled oats (*G) | 125 mL | ¼ cup chopped nuts | 50 mL |

Beat eggs with butter or margarine; beat in honey. (The butter adds flavor and a little additional moistness, but can be omitted.) Add vanilla and rolled oats. Sift in flour, baking powder and salt, then mix in nuts and dates.

Spread in well-buttered 9-inch (22 cm) square pan. Bake in 350°F (180°C) oven for 25–30 minutes, or until mixture draws away from sides of pan. Cool and cut into squares, then roll into balls. If desired, roll in fruit sugar.

Free of: M E W

Can be free of: G C F

Contains: S

# Fruit Torte

Makes 9 servings

| | | | |
|---|---|---|---|
| 1 cup chopped dates, figs, cooked prunes or apricots (*F) | 250 mL | ½ teaspoon soda | 2 mL |
| | | ½ teaspoon salt | 2 mL |
| | | 2 teaspoons grated orange rind (*F) | 10 mL |
| ¼ cup granulated sugar | 60 mL | | |
| | | ½ cup brown sugar | 125 mL |
| ¼ cup fruit juice (*F) or water | 60 mL | ½ cup shortening, softened (*C, F) | 125 mL |
| 2½ cups rolled oats, uncooked (*G) | 625 mL | ¼ cup water | 60 mL |

Combine fruit, granulated sugar and fruit juice. Cook until thick. Cool. Grind oats with fine blade of food chopper.

Mix together ground oats, soda, salt, orange rind and brown sugar. Add shortening and water. Beat until smooth. Divide dough in half. Spread one half of dough in greased 8-inch (20 cm) square pan. Spread with fruit mixture. Roll remaining dough between 2 sheets of waxed paper; chill, remove paper and place dough over filling. Bake in 350°F (180°C) oven for 30 minutes. Cut into squares and serve warm or cold.

Free of: M E W G C

Can be free of: F

Contains: S

# Jelly

| | | | |
|---|---|---|---|
| 1 cup fruit juice (*F) | 250 mL | ¼ cup cold water | 60 mL |
| 1 cup water | 250 mL | 1 envelope unflavored gelatin | |
| 2 tablespoons sugar | 30 mL | | |
| Salt to taste | | | |

Heat fruit juice, water, sugar and salt to boiling point. In a large bowl combine gelatin and cold water. Add boiling mixture and stir until gelatin dissolves. Pour into molds and refrigerate until set. Garnish.

Free of: W G

Can be free of: M C F

Contains: E S

# *Lemon Soufflé*

| | | | |
|---|---|---|---|
| ⅓ cup minute tapioca | 75 mL | 1 teaspoon grated lemon rind | 5 mL |
| ⅔ cup sugar | 150 mL | 2 tablespoons butter or milk-free margarine (*M, C, F) | 30 mL |
| ¼ teaspoon salt | 1 mL | | |
| 1¾ cups water | 425 mL | | |
| 3 tablespoons lemon juice | 50 mL | 3 eggs, separated | |

Combine tapioca, sugar, salt and water. Cook and stir over medium heat until mixture comes to a boil. Stir in lemon juice and rind. Remove from heat and add butter or margarine. Allow to cool slightly. Beat egg whites until stiff. Beat egg yolks until thick and lemon colored. Add tapioca to egg yolks and mix well. Fold into beaten egg whites. Pour into baking dish with straight sides. Place in pan of hot water and bake at 350°F (180°C) for 50–60 minutes, or until soufflé is firm. Serve hot, with a warm fruit sauce.

# Pear Bread

| | | | |
|---|---|---|---|
| 1¾ cups rice flour | 425 mL | ⅓ cup oil (*C, F) | 75 mL |
| 3 heaping teaspoons baking powder | 20 mL | 2½–3 peeled, cored and mashed pears | |
| ½ teaspoon baking soda | 2 mL | ½ teaspoon cinnamon | 2 mL |
| ¾ teaspoon salt | 3 mL | ½ cup nuts (optional) | 125 mL |
| ½ cup sugar or ¼ cup honey (*S) | 125 mL | | |

Mash pears in blender or food processor. Sift dry ingredients into a bowl, then add oil and pears. Mix until blended. Add cinnamon, nuts and pour into a 9 inch × 5 inch (23 cm × 13 cm) loaf pan. Bake at 350°F (180°C) for 45 minutes. Cool for 15 minutes, then remove from pan.

# Tea Loaf

| | | | |
|---|---|---|---|
| 1 cup strong tea | 250 mL | ¼ teaspoon cloves | 1 mL |
| ½ cup raisins (*F) | 125 mL | 1 teaspoon baking soda | 5 mL |
| ⅔ cup rice flour | 150 mL | | |
| ⅓ cup potato flour | 75 mL | 2 teaspoons baking powder | 10 mL |
| ½ cup sugar | 125 mL | | |
| 1 teaspoon cinnamon | 5 mL | ½ teaspoon salt | 2 mL |
| 1 teaspoon nutmeg | 5 mL | ¼ cup shortening (*C, F) | 60 mL |

Add hot tea to raisins and cool. Sift dry ingredients. Add shortening and cut in finely. Add tea mixture and stir only until dry ingredients are moistened. Put into greased small loaf pan and bake at 350°F (180°C) for 40 minutes or until toothpick inserted in centre comes out clean. Cool before slicing.

If following the Feingold diet use dates or nuts instead of raisins.

---

Free of: M E C

Can be free of: W G F

Contains: S

## Bread Pudding

| | | | |
|---|---|---|---|
| ½ cup leftover breadcrumbs (*W, G) from whatever bread allowed | 125 mL | 2 teaspoons vanilla | 10 mL |
| | | 2 tablespoons sugar | 30 mL |
| ½ cup soy milk | 125 mL | Raisins (optional) (*F) | |

Cover crumbs with soy milk. Add vanilla, sugar and raisins. Let sit until milk has been soaked up, adding more milk if necessary. Bake at 325°F (160°C) for 20 minutes. Pour corn or maple syrup on top and serve warm.

---

Free of: M W G C

Contains: E S F

## No-Bake Rice Pudding

| | | | |
|---|---|---|---|
| 2 cups cooked rice | 500 mL | ½ cup raisins (F) (more if desired) | 125 mL |
| 1 extra large egg or 2 small eggs, beaten | | ¼ cup boiling water | 60 mL |
| ½ cup sugar | 125 mL | 1 teaspoon vanilla | 5 mL |

Soak raisins in boiling water. Blend all ingredients and cook in top of a double boiler. Stir occasionally. When mixture coats spoon remove from heat. Keep covered to prevent drying. Serve warm or cooled.

# Applesauce Cake

| | | | | |
|---|---|---|---|---|
| ⅓ cup butter or margarine (*M, C) | 75 mL | 1 teaspoon baking powder (or substitute) | 5 mL |
| ¾ cup honey | 175 mL | 1 cup cold unsweetened apple-sauce | 250 mL |
| 1 beaten egg | | | |
| 2 cups flour (suggest ½ rye (*G) and ½ soy) | 500 mL | 1 cup raisins | 250 mL |
| ½ teaspoon nutmeg | 2 mL | ½ cup nuts (optional) | 125 mL |
| ¼ teaspoon salt | 1 mL | ½ teaspoon cinnamon | 2 mL |
| 1 teaspoon soda | 5 mL | | |

Beat butter, add honey gradually, creaming after each addition. Add egg. Mix and sift dry ingredients and add alternately with apple-sauce to creamed mixture. Fold in raisins and nuts. Pour into well-greased 8 inch square (20 cm × 20 cm) pan. Bake at 350°F (180°C) for approximately 45 minutes or until cake tests done.

# Banana Cake

| | | | | |
|---|---|---|---|---|
| 1 cup mashed bananas | 250 mL | ½ teaspoon baking soda | 2 mL |
| ¼ cup oil (*C, F) | 60 mL | 2 teaspoons baking powder | 10 mL |
| ¾ cup white sugar | 175 mL | | |
| ½ teaspoon vanilla | 2 mL | 1¼ cups plus 2 tablespoons rice flour | 325 mL |
| ¼ teaspoon salt | 1 mL | | |

Blend bananas, oil, sugar and vanilla. Add dry ingredients. Bake in an 8 inch square (20 cm) pan at 375°F (190°C) for 25 minutes. Recipe can be used for cupcakes. Lemon flavored icing is good on this cake.

## Variations

*Jam Squares:* Use banana cake recipe. Put two-thirds batter in an 8 inch (20 cm) square pie pan. Cover with thick jam, mashed cooked cherries, plums, or prunes. Place remaining batter on top. Bake at 375°F (190°C) for 25 minutes.

*Coffee Cake:* Place banana cake batter in pie pan and sprinkle cinnamon mixture on top. Cinnamon mixture consists of: ¼ cup (60 mL) milk-free margarine; ½ cup (125 mL) sugar; ¼ cup (60 mL) rice flour; 1 teaspoon (5 mL) cinnamon. Bake at 375°F (190°C) for 25 minutes.

*Cookies:* To banana cake recipe, add 1 teaspoon (5 mL) molasses, coconut, oatmeal, or raisins. Drop by spoonfuls on cookie sheet and flatten. Bake at 375°F (190°C) about 10 minutes.

**Free of: W G S**

**Can be free of: M E C F**

# *Carrot Cake*

| | | | |
|---|---|---|---|
| 1 cup grated raw carrot | 250 mL | ½ teaspoon cinnamon | 2 mL |
| 1¼ cups rice flour | 300 mL | 2 teaspoons baking powder | 10 mL |
| 1 egg (or egg replacer) (*E) | | 1 teaspoon baking soda | 5 mL |
| ½ cup honey | 125 mL | ¼ cup lemon juice | 60 mL |
| 1 cup melted margarine (*M, C, F) | 250 mL | | |

Preheat oven to 350°F (180°C). Combine all ingredients in a large bowl. Mix well. Pour into a well-buttered 5-cup (1.25 litre) ring mold. Bake at 350°F (180°C) until well done. Let cool 10 minutes before unmolding.

Free of: M W G

Can be free of: C F

Contains: E S

# Chiffon Cake

Makes 9 servings

| | | | |
|---|---|---|---|
| ¾ cup white rice flour | 175 mL | 1 tablespoon lemon juice *or* | 15 mL |
| ¾ cup sugar | 175 mL | 1 teaspoon concentrated lemon juice | 5 mL |
| 1½ teaspoons baking powder | 7 mL | 1 teaspoon lemon peel | 5 mL |
| ½ teaspoon salt | 2 mL | 3 egg whites | |
| ¼ cup oil (*C, F) | 60 mL | 1 teaspoon cream of tartar | 5 mL |
| 3 egg yolks, beaten | | | |
| ¼ cup water | 60 mL | | |

Sift dry ingredients together 3 times. Make a well in dry ingredients and add oil, beaten egg yolks, water, lemon juice, lemon peel. Beat well until smooth, about 5 minutes. Beat egg whites with cream of tartar until stiff but not dry. Fold into batter. Pour into ungreased 8 inch square (20 cm) baking pan. Bake 35 minutes at 350°F (180°C) or until firm to touch. Invert pan on rack to cool. If allowed, top with heated cherry pie filling and whipped cream.

Free of: M E

Can be free of: W G C

Contains: S F

# Heirloom Versatility

| | | | |
|---|---|---|---|
| 1 cup brown sugar | 250 mL | 1¼ cups rice flour *or* | 300 mL |
| 1 cup water | 250 mL | 1½ cups flour (*W, G) | 250 mL |
| 1 cup raisins | 250 mL | ¾ teaspoon baking soda | 3 mL |
| 2 tablespoons drippings, vegetable oil or shortening (*C) | 30 mL | ½ teaspoon ginger | 2 mL |
| ½ teaspoon salt | 2 mL | 1 teaspoon cinnamon | 5 mL |

Over medium heat, cook together until blended the brown sugar, water, raisins, fat and salt. Let cool. Stir in the remaining ingredients and make any of the following versions.

*Cake:* Turn into a greased layer cake pan and bake at 350°F (180°C) for 30 minutes. Mix together ¼ cup (60 mL) margarine or butter, 1 teaspoon (5 mL) vanilla and enough icing sugar for a smooth consistency. Spread over cake.

*Loaf:* Turn into a greased loaf pan and bake at 350°F (180°C) for 1 hour.

*Christmas Cake:* Add chopped dates, 1 cup (250 mL) mixed peel and ½ cup (125 mL) nuts to batter and bake in a greased loaf pan at 350°F (180°C) for 1 hour.

Free of: E W G

Can be free of: M C F

Contains: S

# *Chocolate Date-Nut Cake*

Carob and dates make a good combination.

| | | | |
|---|---|---|---|
| ½ cup boiling water | 125 mL | 1 cup flour— | 250 mL |
| ½ cup chopped dates | 125 mL | ¾ cup (175 mL) brown rice flour and ¼ cup (60 mL) potato flour | |
| 3 tablespoons margarine (*M, C, F) | 50 mL | | |
| ½ cup white sugar | 125 mL | 3 tablespoons cocoa or carob powder | 50 mL |
| ½ teaspoon egg replacer | 2 mL | ¾ teaspoon baking soda | 3 mL |
| and 1 tablespoon water | 15 mL | ½ teaspoon salt | 2 mL |
| 1 teaspoon vanilla | 5 mL | ½ cup chopped walnuts | 125 mL |

Pour boiling water over chopped dates. Cream together margarine, sugar, egg replacer and vanilla. Add cooled date mixture and mix well. Sift together dry ingredients and add to creamed mixture. Beat. Add nuts. Spread in a well-greased 8 inch square (20 cm) pan and bake at 350°F (180°C) for 35 minutes or until toothpick inserted comes out clean.

Free of: M E

Can be free of: C F

Contains: W G S

# Pumpkin Cake

| | | | | |
|---|---|---|---|---|
| ¾ cup shortening (*C, F) | 175 mL | 1 teaspoon baking soda | 5 mL |
| 1 cup brown sugar | 250 mL | ¾ teaspoon cinnamon | 3 mL |
| ½ cup white sugar | 125 mL | ½ teaspoon ginger | 2 mL |
| 2 cups pumpkin | 500 mL | 1 teaspoon salt | 5 mL |
| 2 cups cake flour | 500 mL | ½ cup water | 125 mL |
| 3 teaspoons baking powder | 15 mL | | |

Cream together shortening, sugars and pumpkin. Sift dry ingredients and add to creamed mixture alternately with water. Beat well. Bake at 350°F (180°C) for 30 minutes in greased and floured 9 inch × 13 inch (22 cm × 35 cm) cake pan.

Free of: M E

Can be free of: C F

Contains: W G S

# Double Layer Cake

This recipe can be used with great variety.

| | | | | |
|---|---|---|---|---|
| 2 teaspoons egg replacer | 10 mL | 1 teaspoon salt | 5 mL |
| 4 tablespoons water | 50 mL | ½ cup shortening (*C, F) | 125 mL |
| 2½ cups cake flour | 625 mL | 1 cup water | 250 mL |
| 1½ cups sugar | 375 mL | 1 teaspoon vanilla | 5 mL |
| 3 teaspoons baking powder | 15 mL | | |

Mix egg replacer and water well. Sift dry ingredients together. Mix shortening, water and vanilla with egg replacer. Beat well, adding dry ingredients gradually. Pour into two 8 inch square (20 cm) layer cake pans and bake at 375°F (190°C) for 30–35 minutes.

## Variations

### Pineapple Upside-Down Cake

|   |   |   |
|---|---|---|
| 1 | recipe double layer cake | |
| 3 | tablespoons butter (*M) | 40 mL |
| ½ | cup brown sugar | 125 mL |
| 6 | slices pineapple | |
| 6 | maraschino cherries (*F optional) | |

Melt butter in 9 inch (23 cm) square cake pan. Sprinkle with brown sugar and heat until bubbly. Remove from heat and arrange pineapple and cherries in butterscotch mixture. Spread layer cake batter over fruit. Bake at 350°F (180°C) for 45–50 minutes. Turn out onto plate with pineapple side up. Serve plain or with whipped cream.

### Dutch Apple Cake

|   |   |   |
|---|---|---|
| 1 | recipe double layer cake | |
| 4 | medium-sized apples | |
| ⅓ | cup brown sugar | 75 mL |
| ½ | teaspoon cinnamon | 2 mL |

Grease an 8 inch (20 cm) square pan. Peel, core and slice apples into a bowl. Mix brown sugar and cinnamon and mix with apples. Spread half the batter in prepared pan. Cover with about half the sliced apples. Spread on remaining batter. Arrange balance of apple slices on top. Bake at 350°F (180°C) for 45–50 minutes.

*Dutch Peach Cake*

>      1 recipe double layer cake
>      1 can peaches drained
>      ¼ cup sugar            60 mL
>      ¾ teaspoon cinnamon    3 mL

Pour double layer cake batter into a greased 9 inch (23 cm) square pan. Cut each drained peach half into 4 or 5 slices. Arrange slices over top of batter, slightly pressing in cut edges. Sprinkle with sugar-cinnamon mixture. Bake in preheated oven for 30–40 minutes at 400°F (200°C). Serve warm, either plain or with whipped cream.

| Free of: M W G C |
| --- |
| Can be free of: F |
| Contains: E S |

# *Potato Cake*

| | | | |
| --- | --- | --- | --- |
| ¾ cup sifted potato flour | 175 mL | ¾ cup sugar | 175 mL |
| 1 teaspoon baking powder | 5 mL | 1 teaspoon vanilla | 5 mL |
| ½ teaspoon salt | 2 mL | 1 teaspoon lemon juice *or* | 5 mL |
| 4 eggs | | ½ teaspoon almond extract (*F) | 2 mL |

Sift flour, baking powder and salt; set aside. Mix eggs and sugar into another bowl and place the bowl into another of hot water. Beat until mixture is lukewarm. Remove from hot water and continue beating 6–8 minutes or until mixture resembles whipped cream. Add vanilla, lemon juice and extract. Gradually add dry ingredients to egg mixture. Carefully pour into an ungreased tube pan. Bake at 350°F (180°C) about 40 minutes. Invert and suspend until cool.

Free of: W G C

Can be free of: F

Contains: M E S

# Sponge Cake

Hard work but worth it!

| | | Topping | |
|---|---|---|---|
| 6 eggs (at room temperature) | | 1 10-ounce package frozen raspberries (thawed) (*F) | 284 g |
| 1 cup sugar | 250 mL | | |
| ½ cup powdered skim milk | 125 mL | ½ cup orange juice (*F) | 125 mL |
| 1 tablespoon lemon juice | 15 mL | 1 cup whipping cream | 250 mL |
| ½ teaspoon salt | 2 mL | 1–2 teaspoons sugar | 5–10 mL |
| 1 cup rice flour | 250 mL | | |

Blend first five ingredients in large bowl. Beat at high speed, until mixture holds in soft peaks, 15–20 minutes. Beat rice flour, a tablespoon at a time into mixture. Scrape sides of bowl often. Rinse a 10-inch (25 cm) tube pan with cold water. Pour batter into pan and bake 50–60 minutes at 350°F (180°C). Cake surface should spring back when gently pressed. Turn pan upside down. Remove cake when cool and place on plate.

About an hour before serving, thoroughly drain juice from berries. Mix this juice with orange juice. Spoon juices over cake and let soak in; be careful not to saturate cake too much. Whip cream, adding sugar if desired. Frost top and sides of cake. Drain berries on paper towelling. Decorate top of cake with the berries.

Free of: M E

Can be free of: C F

Contains: W G S

# Snacking Cake

| | | | | |
|---|---|---|---|---|
| 1½ cups sifted flour | 375 mL | | 1½ teaspoons vanilla | 7 mL |
| 4 tablespoons cocoa | 60 mL | | 1 tablespoon vinegar or lemon concentrate | 15 mL |
| 1 teaspoon baking powder | 5 mL | | 5 tablespoons oil or shortening (*C, F) | 75 mL |
| 1 teaspoon baking soda | 5 mL | | 1 cup lukewarm water | 250 mL |
| ½ teaspoon salt | 2 mL | | | |
| 1 cup fine white sugar | 250 mL | | | |

Sift dry ingredients into an ungreased 8 inch (20 cm) square pan. Make 3 holes equally spaced in the mixture. Pour vanilla into one, vinegar into another, and oil in the third. Pour water over top and stir well. Bake at 325°F (160°C) for 45–50 minutes.

Free of: M E W G

Can be free of: C F

Contains: S

# White Cake

| | | | | |
|---|---|---|---|---|
| 3 tablespoons oil (*C, F) | 40 mL | | 1 tablespoon baking powder | 15 mL |
| ¾ cup white sugar | 175 mL | | ½ teaspoon salt | 2 mL |
| ⅔ cup rice or soy flour | 150 mL | | ⅓ cup water | 75 mL |
| ⅓ cup potato flour | 75 mL | | 1 teaspoon vanilla | 5 mL |

Mix oil and sugar. Sift dry ingredients and add to first mixture alternately with water. Stir in vanilla. Turn into a greased 8 inch square (20 cm) cake pan and bake at 350°F (180°C) for 30–35 minutes.

Free of: E W G C S F

Contains: M

# Creamy Frosting

| | | | |
|---|---|---|---|
| 1 teaspoon unflavored gelatin | 5 mL | 1 teaspoon vanilla | 5 mL |
| 1 cup whipping cream | 250 mL | 3 tablespoons honey | 40 mL |

Place gelatin in pan with 1 tablespoon (15 mL) cold water. Put pan on stove over medium heat and stir until gelatin is dissolved. Beat whipping cream until thick and fluffy. Scrape gelatin into whipping cream, add honey and vanilla. Beat and mix well. Frost cake. Refrigerate if not used immediately.

Free of: M W G F

Contains: E C S

# Fluffy Frosting

| | | | |
|---|---|---|---|
| 2 egg whites | | 2 teaspoons cornstarch | 10 mL |
| 1 tablespoon vinegar | 15 mL | | |
| 1 teaspoon lemon juice | 5 mL | 2½ cups icing sugar | 625 mL |
| Pinch of salt | | | |

Beat egg whites until stiff but not dry. Add vinegar, lemon juice, salt and cornstarch. Continue beating. Gradually add icing sugar until mixture can be spread. Frost cake, heaping high in centre of cake. Decorate as desired. Refrigerate.

Free of: E W G

Can be free of: M F

Contains: C S

# *Butterless Butter Icing*

| | | | |
|---|---|---|---|
| 1 tablespoon milk-free margarine (*M, F) | 15 mL | ¼ cup water or juice | 60 mL |
| 1 teaspoon vanilla | 5 mL | 2½ cup icing sugar | 625 mL |

Soften margarine, add vanilla and water. Add half of icing sugar and mix. Continue to add icing sugar until a thick, smooth consistency is reached.

### Variation
Add 2 tablespoons (25 mL) cocoa for chocolate icing.

Free of: M E W G C F

Contains: S

# *Lemon Pie Filling*

| | | | |
|---|---|---|---|
| package egg replacer | | ⅓ cup lemon juice | 75 mL |
| 1 cup sugar | 250 mL | 2 tablespoons grated lemon rind | 25 mL |
| ¼ teaspoon salt | 1 mL | 1 baked 9-inch (23 cm) pie shell, as allowed | |
| 1½ cups hot water | 375 mL | | |

Combine egg replacer, sugar and salt in double boiler and stir until blended. Add water, lemon juice and rind and stir over medium heat until smooth and thick. Remove from heat and stir for 5 minutes to cool. Pour into allowed pie shell. Refrigerate 2 hours before serving. Top with whipped cream if allowed.

# Custard Pie

| | | | | |
|---|---|---|---|---|
| 1 | unbaked 8–9 inch (23–25 cm) allowed pie crust | | 4 teaspoons egg replacer | 20 mL |
| 1 | cup sweetened condensed milk (*M, C) | 250 mL | 8 tablespoons water | 120 mL |
| 1½ | cups hot water | 375 mL | 1 teaspoon nutmeg (optional) | 5 mL |
| ¼ | teaspoon salt | 1 mL | | |
| 1 | teaspoon vanilla | 5 mL | | |

Combine all ingredients in a blender and whip until smooth. Pour into unbaked pie crust and sprinkle with nutmeg. Bake for 30–35 minutes at 325°F (160°C) or until knife inserted comes out clean. Cool and refrigerate.

## Variation

For coconut custard pie add 1½ cups (375 mL) shredded coconut to liquid mixture after blending, then follow the baking instructions above.

# Yogurt-Cheese Pie

| | | | |
|---|---|---|---|
| 8 ounces soft cream cheese | 227 g | 1 teaspoon vanilla | 5 mL |
| ⅔ cup yogurt | 150 mL | 6 dates, chopped | |
| 1 tablespoon honey | 15 mL | | |

Beat together cream cheese, yogurt, honey and vanilla until very smooth. Stir in dates and pour into a prepared 9-inch (23 cm) pie shell. Refrigerate several hours. Goes well with oat pie crust (see p. 100).

| Free of: E W G F |
| Can be free of: C |
| Contains: M S |

# Chocolate Cream Pie

1 baked 8–9 inch (23–25 cm) allowed pie crust, crumb or nut crust
2 squares unsweetened chocolate
1 can sweetened condensed milk (*C)    300 mL

3 tablespoons hot water    40 mL
⅛ teaspoon salt    .5 mL
1 teaspoon vanilla    5 mL
1 cup whipping cream    250 mL

Melt chocolate in a double boiler with milk, water and salt, stirring over medium heat until thick and bubbling. Remove from heat and add vanilla. Cool. Whip cream until peaks form and fold cream into cooled chocolate mixture. Turn cream-chocolate mixture into prepared pie shell and refrigerate at least 2 hours before serving.

| Free of: E W G S |
| Can be free of: M C F |

# Coconut Pie Crust

2 cups flaked coconut    500 mL

¼ cup butter or milk-free margarine (*M, C, F)    50 mL

Lightly brown coconut in margarine over medium heat. Press mixture into bottom and sides of a greased 8 inch (20 cm) pie tin. Cool. Two tablespoons (25 mL) of the mixture may be reserved to garnish pie.

Free of: E

Can be free of: M W G C F

Contains: S

# *Crumb Pie Crust*

Suitable for cheese cake or cream fillings.

| | | | |
|---|---|---|---|
| 1⅓ cups cookie or cake crumbs (to suit your particular diet) (*W, G) | 325 mL | ¼ cup soft butter or milk-free margarine (*M, C, F) | 60 mL |
| | | 1 tablespoon sugar | 15 mL |

Mix cookie crumbs, margarine and sugar together. Line 9-inch (23 cm) pie pan, saving some crumb mixture for topping.

Free of: E W G

Can be free of: M F

Contains: S C

# *Cornflake Pie Crust*

| | | | |
|---|---|---|---|
| 1 cup cornflake crumbs | 250 mL | 2 tablespoons melted milk-free margarine (*M, F) | 25 mL |
| 1 tablespoon sugar | 15 mL | | |

Toss together cornflake crumbs, sugar and margarine until crumbs are thoroughly coated. Press the mixture evenly and firmly onto bottom and up sides of an 8-inch (20 cm) pie pan; bake 8 minutes at 375°F (190°C).

Free of: M E W C S

Can be free of: G F

# Oat Pie Crust

| ½ cup rolled oats (*G) | 125 mL | 2 tablespoons safflower oil (*F) | 25 mL |
| ½ cup pitted dates | 125 mL | | |

Place oats and pitted dates through fine blade of a food grinder. Mix with oil and press into an 8-inch (20 cm) pie pan to make a pie shell.

Free of: M W G C F

Contains: E S

# Meringue Shell

| 3 egg whites | | Dash of salt | |
| 1 teaspoon vanilla | 5 mL | 1 cup sugar | 250 mL |
| ¼ teaspoon cream of tartar | 1 mL | | |

Have egg whites at room temperature. Add vanilla, cream of tartar and salt. Beat until frothy. Gradually add sugar, a small amount at a time, beating until peaks are very stiff and sugar is dissolved.

Cover cookie sheets with plain ungreased paper. Using a 9-inch (23 cm) pie plate as guide, draw circle on paper. Spread meringue over circle; shape into shell with back of spoon, making bottom ½ inch (1.25 cm) thick and mounding around edge to make sides 1¾ inches (4 cm) high. Bake at 275°F (140°C) for 1 hour. Turn off heat and let dry in oven with the door closed for at least 2 hours.

For individual meringue shells draw 8 3⅓-inch circles; spread eight with about ⅓ cup (75 mL) of meringue. Shape with spoon to make shells. Bake as above.

Free of: M E W G C

Contains: S F

# Ground Almond Pie Crust

| | | | |
|---|---|---|---|
| 1½ cups finely ground unblanched almonds (F) | 375 mL | 4 teaspoons granulated sugar | 20 mL |

Mix well and press into 9-inch (23 cm) pie plate. Bake at 350°F (180°C) for 10 minutes.

Free of: M E W G S

Can be free of: C F

# Brown Rice-Flour Pie Crust

Makes 1 double 9-inch (23 cm) pie crust

| | | | |
|---|---|---|---|
| 1½ cups brown rice flour | 350 mL | ⅔ cup vegetable shortening (*C, F) | 150 mL |
| ¼ cup potato flour | 60 mL | ½ cup ice water | 125 mL |
| ½ teaspoon salt | 2 mL | Soy milk | |
| | | Sugar | |

Sift flours and salt together in a bowl. Cut in shortening and blend well. Add ice water a little at a time, blending thoroughly after each addition until dough forms a ball and leaves sides of bowl. Roll out on waxpaper and place in pie plate. Brush top of pie crust with soy milk and sprinkle with sugar before baking. Bake at 425°F (220°C) for 10–15 minutes until golden brown.

| Free of: E W |
| --- |
| Can be free of: M C F |
| Contains: G S |

# Rye Cracker Crumb Pie Crust

| | | | |
| --- | --- | --- | --- |
| 15 rye crackers | | 2 teaspoons hot | 10 mL |
| ¼ cup sugar | 60 mL | water | |
| ⅓ cup margarine (*M, C, F) | 75 mL | | |

Grease an 8-inch (20 cm) pie plate. Roll crackers fine enough to make 1 cup (250 mL) of crumbs. Combine crumbs and sugar. Add margarine and water. Blend thoroughly. Press crumbs evenly and firmly onto the bottom and sides of pie plate. Form an edge around top of crust, not on rim of plate. Chill thoroughly. Fill with a fruit, cornstarch gelatin filling or ice cream. Place pie plate in hot water for a minute before cutting.

| Free of: M E W |
| --- |
| Can be free of: G C |
| Contains: S F |

# Applesauce Cookies

Makes about 5 dozen cookies

| | | | |
| --- | --- | --- | --- |
| 1 cup brown sugar | 250 mL | 1 teaspoon vanilla | 5 mL |
| ¾ cup oil (*C) | 175 mL | 4 cups rolled oats (*G) | 1000 mL |
| 1 cup thick applesauce (F) | 250 mL | ½ cup chopped dates | 125 mL |
| ½ cup chopped nuts | 125 mL | | |
| ½ teaspoon sea salt | 2 mL | | |

Preheat oven to 375°F (190°C). Beat brown sugar and oil together. Add the remaining ingredients and mix well. Drop from a teaspoon onto an oiled baking sheet. Bake for 25 minutes or until well browned. Cool on the sheet.

## Variation

If substituting honey for sugar either decrease amount of applesauce or increase the amount of rolled oats.

Free of: M E

Can be free of: C F

Contains: W G S

# Chocolate Chip Cookies

| | | | | |
|---|---|---|---|---|
| ½ | cup shortening (*C, F) | 125 mL | ½ cup water or juice | 125 mL |
| ¼ | cup brown sugar | 60 mL | ½ cup nuts as allowed | 125 mL |
| ¾ | cup white sugar | 175 mL | 6 ounces unsweetened milk-free chocolate chips | 170 g |
| 1 | teaspoon vanilla | 5 mL | | |
| 2 | cups flour | 500 mL | | |
| ¾ | teaspoon soda | 3 mL | | |
| ½ | teaspoon baking powder | 2 mL | | |

Cream shortening; add sugars and vanilla. Add sifted dry ingredients alternately with water. Stir in nuts and chocolate chips. Bake at 350°F (180°C) for 10 minutes.

## Variation

To replace chocolate and/or nuts, use rind of half an orange and ¾ cup (175 mL) raisins. This is not suitable for those on the Feingold diet.

## Chocolate Drops

Free of: M E

Can be free of: W G F

Contains: C S

| | | | |
|---|---|---|---|
| ¼ cup shortening (*F) | 60 mL | ½ cup cocoa | 125 mL |
| 1 cup sugar | 250 mL | 4 teaspoons double-acting baking powder | 20 mL |
| 1 teaspoon salt | 5 mL | ¼ cup cornstarch | 60 mL |
| 2 teaspoons vanilla | 10 mL | 2 cups sifted wheat (*W, G) or rice flour | 500 mL |
| ¾ cup soy milk (undiluted) | 175 mL | | |

Preheat oven to 375°F (190°C). Mix shortening, sugar, salt, and vanilla until smooth and creamy. Measure 2 tablespoons (25 mL) soy milk and add to creamed mixture along with cocoa, baking powder and cornstarch. Add flour alternately with remaining soy milk.

Shape dough in balls the size of walnuts and bake 7–10 minutes on greased cookie sheet.

## Sugarless Cookies

Free of: E W G S

Can be free of: M C F

| | | | |
|---|---|---|---|
| ¾ cup soy flour | 175 mL | ⅓ cup milk-free margarine (*M, C, F) | 75 mL |
| ½ cup potato flour | 125 mL | ⅓ cup honey | 75 mL |
| 3 tablespoons baking powder | 40 mL | ¼ teaspoon vanilla | 1 mL |
| | | Water, as needed | |

Sift dry ingredients together 4 times. Cream margarine, honey and vanilla. Add dry ingredients. Batter may require up to ½ cup (125 mL) water to moisten it to drop-cookie consistency. Drop spoonfuls onto ungreased cookie sheet. Bake at 350°F (180°C) for 10 minutes. These burn easily—watch them carefully.

## Chocolate Wafer Cookies

Makes 4 dozen cookies

Free of: E W

Can be free of: M C F

Contains: S G

| | | | | |
|---|---|---|---|---|
| ¾ cup butter or milk-free margarine (*M, C, F) | 175 mL | ¾ cup cocoa or carob powder | 175 mL | |
| 1 cup white sugar | 250 mL | 1 teaspoon baking powder | 5 mL | |
| 1 teaspoon vanilla | 5 mL | ½ teaspoon baking soda | 2 mL | |
| 1 cup brown rice flour | 250 mL | ½ teaspoon salt | 2 mL | |
| 1 cup rye flour | 250 mL | ¼ cup milk or soy milk | 60 mL | |

Cream butter and sugar well and add vanilla. Sift together dry ingredients and add to creamed mixture alternately with milk. Mix thoroughly. Shape into two 10 inch × 1½ inch (25 cm × 4 cm) rolls. Wrap in wax paper. Chill overnight. Slice thinly and bake on an ungreased cookie sheet at 350°F (180°C) for 10 minutes. Remove from cookie sheet immediately.

## Frying Pan Dates

Free of: M W G C F

Contains: E S

| | | | |
|---|---|---|---|
| 1½ cups chopped dates | 375 mL | ½ teaspoon salt | 2 mL |
| 2 eggs, beaten | | 2 cups rice krispies | 500 mL |
| 1 teaspoon vanilla | 5 mL | Chopped nuts, coconut | |
| 1 cup white sugar | 250 mL | | |

Mix dates, eggs, vanilla, sugar and salt together and cook for ten minutes in heavy frying pan, stirring *all* the time. Add rice krispies. Form into small balls and roll in chopped nuts or coconut.

| Free of: E W G |
| Can be free of: F |
| Contains: M C S |

# Cornmeal Cookies

Makes 2 dozen cookies

| | | | | |
|---|---|---|---|---|
| ¼ cup oil (*F) | 60 mL | ½ teaspoon salt | 2 mL |
| ½ cup brown sugar | 125 mL | ¼ teaspoon cinnamon | 1 mL |
| 1½ cups cornstarch | 375 mL | (optional) | |
| ¼–½ cup cornmeal | 60–125 mL | ½ cup milk | 125 mL |
| 1½ teaspoons baking powder | 7 mL | | |

Combine oil and brown sugar. Add remaining dry ingredients and mix well. Add milk and beat thoroughly. Drop by spoonfuls onto greased cookie sheet. Bake at 375°F (190°C) about 15 minutes. Remove from cookie sheet immediately.

| Free of: M E W |
| Can be free of: C F |
| Contains: G S |

# Pineapple Drop Cookies

| | | | | |
|---|---|---|---|---|
| ½ cup shortening (*C, F) | 125 mL | 1 cup potato starch | 250 mL |
| ½ cup brown sugar | 125 mL | 3 teaspoons baking powder | 15 mL |
| ½ cup white sugar | 125 mL | ¼ teaspoon baking soda | 1 mL |
| ½ cup drained crushed pineapple | 125 mL | ¼ teaspoon salt | 1 mL |
| 1 cup barley flour | 250 mL | ½ cup chopped nuts | 125 mL |

Cream shortening and sugars and add crushed pineapple. Combine dry ingredients and add to mixture. When well mixed, add nuts. Drop onto well-greased cookie sheet and bake at 350°F (180°C) for about 12 minutes or until lightly browned. Remove to rack to cool.

Free of: E W G

Can be free of: M C F

Contains: S

# *Fudge Cookies*

| | | | |
|---|---|---|---|
| 2 cups white sugar | 500 mL | 6 tablespoons cocoa | 90 mL |
| ½ cup milk-free margarine (*M, C, F) | 125 mL | or carob powder Pinch salt | |
| ½ cup water | 125 mL | 4 cups puffed rice | 1000 mL |
| | | 1 teaspoon vanilla | 5 mL |

Mix sugar, margarine, water, cocoa and salt. Bring to a rolling boil. Remove from stove and add vanilla and cereal. Mix well. Drop by tablespoons onto waxed paper. Cool.

## *Variation*
If allowed, 1 cup (250 mL) coconut can be substituted for one cup of cereal.

Free of: E W G

Can be free of: M F

Contains: C S

# *French Lace Cookies*
Makes 72 cookies

| | | | |
|---|---|---|---|
| 1 cup rice flour | 250 mL | ¼ cup shortening (*F) | 60 mL |
| 1 cup finely chopped almonds (not blanched) (*F) | 250 mL | ⅔ cup brown sugar, packed | 150 mL |
| ¼ cup butter, or milk-free margarine (*M, F) | 60 mL | ½ cup corn syrup | 125 mL |

Mix together the rice flour and chopped nuts. Mix butter, shortening, sugar and corn syrup. Bring to boil, stirring. Remove from heat. Stir into flour and almond mixture. Drop by ½ teaspoons (2 mL) onto well-greased baking sheet, 3 inches (8 cm) apart. Bake at 325°F (160°C) for 8–10 minutes. Let cool 1 minute, lift off cookie sheet onto a paper towel to absorb excess oil. Store in airtight jar.

Free of: M E S

Can be free of: C F

Contains: W G

# Oatmeal Cookies

Makes 6 dozen cookies

| | | | | |
|---|---|---|---|---|
| 2 cups flour | 500 mL | ½ cup coconut | 125 mL |
| ½ teaspoon salt | 2 mL | 1 cup shortening | 250 mL |
| 1 teaspoon baking soda | 5 mL | (*C, F) | |
| 2 cups rolled oats | 500 mL | ¾ cup maple syrup | 175 mL |
| | | 1 teaspoon vanilla | 5 mL |

Sift flour, salt, and baking soda together. Mix in oats and coconut. Cream shortening and maple syrup well. Mix in vanilla. Add flour mixture to shortening mixture, a part at a time, mixing well after each addition. **Note:** If dough is too dry and falling apart add up to ¼ cup (60 mL) of warm water.

Drop dough by small spoonfuls, well spaced, onto a greased cookie sheet. Flatten each mound with a fork dipped in water in a criss-cross pattern. Bake at 350°F (180°C) for 12–15 minutes.

### Variation
If allowed, sandwich with a date filling.

Free of: M W G C

Can be free of: F

Contains: E S

# Meringue Cookies

Makes about 4 dozen cookies

| | | | |
|---|---|---|---|
| 2 egg whites | | ½ teaspoon vanilla | 2 mL |
| ½ cup fine sugar | 125 mL | Dates, chocolate chips or raisins (*F) | |

Beat egg whites until stiff. Add sugar by tablespoons. Add vanilla. Add raisins, dates or chocolate chips. Place by teaspoonfuls onto brown paper on a cookie sheet. Bake 20 minutes at 350°F (180°C).

# Peanut Butter Meringues

Makes about 3½ dozen cookies

| | | | |
|---|---|---|---|
| 2 egg whites | | ¾ cup peanut | 175 mL |
| ¼ teaspoon salt | 1 mL | butter (*C, F) | |
| ¾ cup sugar | 175 mL | | |

Beat egg whites until soft peaks form. Add salt and sugar gradually. Beat in peanut butter carefully; do not overbeat. Drop by teaspoons onto a greased cookie sheet. Bake at 325°F (160°C) for approximately 20 minutes.

free of: M W G

Can be free of: C F

Contains: E S

free of: M E

Can be free of: C F

Contains: W G S

# Pumpkin Nut Cookies

Makes 4 dozen cookies

| | | | |
|---|---|---|---|
| ½ cup oil (*C, F) | 125 mL | 1 teaspoon salt | 5 mL |
| ½ cup brown sugar | 125 mL | 3 teaspoons cinnamon | 15 mL |
| ½ cup honey | 125 mL | ½ teaspoon nutmeg | 2 mL |
| 1 cup cooked pumpkin | 250 mL | ¼ teaspoon cloves | 1 mL |
| 1½ cups all-purpose flour | 375 mL | 1 cup chopped walnuts | 250 mL |
| ½ cup soy flour | 125 mL | 1 cup chopped dates or raisins (*F) | 250 mL |
| 4 teaspoons baking powder | 20 mL | | |

Cream oil, sugar, honey and pumpkin. Sift together all of the dry ingredients. Add dry ingredients to creamed mixture and beat until smooth. Add chopped nuts and fruit and blend thoroughly. Drop by teaspoonfuls onto greased cookie sheets and bake at 350°F (180°C) for 10–15 minutes or until firm.

Free of: M E

Can be free of: C F

Contains: W G S

# Pumpkin Cookies

| | | | |
|---|---|---|---|
| 1 cup sugar | 250 mL | 1 teaspoon baking soda | 5 mL |
| ½ cup shortening (*C, F) | 125 mL | 1 teaspoon baking powder | 5 mL |
| 1 cup pumpkin | 250 mL | 1 teaspoon cinnamon | 5 mL |
| 1 teaspoon vanilla | 5 mL | 1 cup raisins (*F) | 250 mL |
| ½ teaspoon salt, or slightly more | 2 mL | ½ cup nuts (optional) | 125 mL |
| 1 cup rice flour | 250 mL | | |
| ¾ cup potato flour | 175 mL | | |

Cream sugar and shortening, add pumpkin, vanilla and salt. Sift flours, soda, baking powder and cinnamon. Add to creamed mixture. Fold in raisins and nuts. Drop by teaspoonfuls onto greased cookie sheet. Bake at 350°F (180°C) until done, about 10 minutes.

Free of: E W G

Can be free of: F

Contains: M C S

# Melt-in-Your-Mouth Shortbread

Makes about 3 dozen

| | | | |
|---|---|---|---|
| ½ cup cornstarch | 125 mL | 1 cup rice flour | 250 mL |
| ½ cup icing sugar | 125 mL | ¾ cup butter (*F) | 175 mL |

Sift cornstarch, icing sugar and rice flour together. Add butter. Mix with hands until a soft smooth dough forms. Refrigerate one hour. Shape dough into 1 inch (2.5 cm) balls. Place about 1½ inches (4 cm) apart on ungreased cookie sheet; flatten with a lightly floured fork. Bake at 300°F (150°C) for 20–25 minutes or until edges are lightly browned.

## Variations

Form balls as above. Roll in finely crushed corn flakes or crushed nuts as allowed. Press top of ball with thumb. Add a dab of red jelly if allowed.

Mix in 2 tablespoons finely chopped peel, and 2 tablespoons finely crushed nuts as allowed. Flatten with a lightly floured fork.

Free of: W G

Can be free of: M C F

Contains: E S

# Toll House Cookies

| | | | |
|---|---|---|---|
| ¾ cup soy flour | 175 mL | 6 tablespoons sugar | 90 mL |
| ¼ cup potato starch flour | 60 mL | 6 tablespoons brown sugar | 90 mL |
| ½ teaspoon salt | 2 mL | ½ teaspoon vanilla | 2 mL |
| ½ teaspoon baking soda | 2 mL | ¼ teaspoon water | 1 mL |
| ½ cup milk-free margarine (*M, C, F) | 125 mL | 1 egg | |
| | | Chocolate pieces (*M) | |
| | | ½ cup chopped nuts | 125 mL |

Sift together flours, salt and baking soda. Blend margarine, sugars, vanilla and water. Beat in egg. Add flour mixture and mix well. Stir in chocolate pieces and chopped nuts. Drop by well-rounded teaspoonfuls onto cookie sheet. Bake 10–12 minutes at 375°F (190°C).

Free of: E W G

Can be free of: M

Contains: C S F

# Apricot Bars

| | | | |
|---|---|---|---|
| 1 cup sifted rice flour | 250 mL | ¼ cup oil or melted milk-free margarine (*M) | 60 mL |
| ¼ cup cornstarch | 60 mL | 1 cup dried apricots, diced | 250 mL |
| 2 teaspoons baking powder | 10 mL | ¾ cup milk or soy milk (*M) | 175 mL |
| ½ teaspoon salt | 2 mL | | |
| 1 cup brown sugar | 250 mL | | |

Sift rice flour, cornstarch, baking powder and salt together. Mix sugar, margarine and apricots. Blend two mixtures together and add milk gradually, mixing well. Use a 9 inch × 9 inch × 2 inch (23 × 23 × 5 cm) pan. Bake at 375°F (190°C) for 25–30 minutes. Cut into bars.

Free of: M W G

Can be free of: C F

Contains: E S

# Blonde Brownies

| | | | |
|---|---|---|---|
| ⅓ cup shortening (*C, F) | 75 mL | 1 teaspoon baking powder | 5 mL |
| 1½ cups packed brown sugar | 375 mL | ½ teaspoon salt | 2 mL |
| 2 eggs, beaten | | ½ cup unsweetened chocolate chips | 125 mL |
| 1 teaspoon vanilla | 5 mL | 1 cup chopped walnuts | 250 mL |
| 1 cup sifted rice flour | 250 mL | | |

Melt shortening, stir in sugar, eggs and vanilla. Sift flour, baking powder and salt into shortening mix and blend well. Stir in floured nuts and chocolate chips. Spread into 9 inch square (23 cm) pan. Bake about 30 minutes at 350°F (180°C) in pan. Cool to luke-warm, then spread with browned butter icing (p. 113). Cut into bars.

# Bikini Bars

| | | | |
|---|---|---|---|
| ⅔ cup (½ 15-ounce can) sweetened condensed milk (*M, C) | 150 mL | ½ cup chopped nuts | 125 mL |
| 1 teaspoon vanilla | 5 mL | ¼ cup finely chopped maraschino cherries | 60 mL |
| Salt to taste | | Butter icing or icing suitable to diet | |
| 2½ cups desiccated coconut | 625 mL | 1 square unsweetened chocolate | |
| 2 cups chopped dates or raisins | 500 mL | | |

Preheat oven to 350°F (180°C). Stir condensed milk, vanilla and salt together. Add coconut, dates or raisins, nuts and cherries. Mix. Spoon into an 8 inch × 8 inch × 2 inch (20 × 20 × 5 cm) pan which has been greased, lined with paper and greased again. Cook 30 minutes. Cool 2–3 minutes before removing from pan; peel off paper; cool.

Ice with browned butter icing (see below). Melt chocolate over hot water and drizzle over. Cut into finger-length bars.

# Browned Butter Icing

| | | | |
|---|---|---|---|
| 1½ tablespoons butter (*F) | 25 mL | ¾ teaspoon vanilla | 3 mL |
| 1½ cups sifted icing sugar | 350 mL | 1½ tablespoons light cream | 25 mL |

Place butter in small saucepan and heat until golden brown. Add icing sugar, vanilla and enough cream to make mixture easy to spread.

# Fudge Squares

Free of: M W G

Can be free of: C F

Contains: E S

| | |
|---|---|
| 1 cup sugar | 250 mL |
| ½ cup milk-free margarine (*C, F) | 125 mL |
| 4 eggs | |
| 1 teaspoon vanilla | 5 mL |
| 2 squares unsweetened melted chocolate | |
| ½ cup brown rice flour | 125 mL |
| 1 teaspoon baking powder | 5 mL |
| ¼ teaspoon salt | 1 mL |
| 1½ cups chopped walnuts | 375 mL |
| ½ cup raisins | 125 mL |

Preheat oven to 350°F (180°C). Cream sugar and margarine. Add eggs, vanilla and melted chocolate and beat until light and fluffy. Sift together flour, baking powder and salt and add to creamed mixture, blending well. Mix in nuts and raisins. Spread into an 8 inch (20 cm) square cake pan that has been greased and floured. Bake for 25 minutes or until knife inserted comes out clean.

# Frosted Brownies

Free of: M W G

Can be free of: C F

Contains: E S

| | |
|---|---|
| ¼ cup milk-free margarine (*C, F) | 60 mL |
| 1 cup white sugar | 250 mL |
| 2 eggs | |
| 1 teaspoon vanilla | 5 mL |
| 1 cup flour, ½ cup (125 mL) rice flour and ½ cup (125 mL) potato flour | 250 mL |
| ½ teaspoon baking powder | 2 mL |
| 2 tablespoons cocoa or carob powder | 25 mL |
| ¼ teaspoon salt | 1 mL |
| ¼ cup water | 60 mL |
| ½ cup chopped nuts | 125 mL |

Cream margarine, sugar; add eggs and vanilla and beat until fluffy. Sift together dry ingredients and add to creamed mixture alternately with water. Mix well. Add nuts. Bake at 375°F (190°C) in a greased 8 inch (20 cm) square pan for 25 minutes.

## Frosting

| | |
|---|---|
| 1½ teaspoons margarine | 7 mL |
| ½ teaspoon vanilla | 2 mL |
| 1½ tablespoons cocoa or carob powder | 22 mL |
| 1 tablespoon hot coffee | 15 mL |
| ⅔ cup icing sugar | 150 mL |

Beat ingredients together well; frost brownies while still warm.

Free of: M W G S

Can be free of: C

Contains: E F

# Strawberry Ice Cream

Makes 4 servings

| | | | |
|---|---|---|---|
| 2 cups strawberries | 500 mL | ½ cup chilled oil (*C) | 125 mL |
| 1 cup honey | 250 mL | 2 egg yolks | |
| 1 cup ice-cold water | 250 mL | | |
| 1 cup soy milk powder | 250 mL | | |

Combine strawberries and honey. Cover and chill in the refrigerator for 1 hour or more. Place the water and soy milk powder in the blender. Blend until smooth and thick. Add oil slowly while blending at high speed. Add the egg yolks and blend well. Add the strawberry mixture and blend again. Pour into chilled ice cube trays and freeze until the mixture is solid around the edges, and slightly mushy in the middle. Turn into blender and blend until smooth. Return to trays and freeze again. Repeat the freezing and blending 2 times more and then serve frozen.

| Free of: M E W G S | |
| --- | --- |
| Can be free of: C | |
| Contains: F | |

# Frozen Dessert

Serves 6–8

| 2 cups soy milk | 500 mL | ¼ cup flax seeds | 60 mL |
| 1 cup almonds | 250 mL | (if desired) | |
| 1 cup pecans | 250 mL | ½ cup honey | 125 mL |
| ½ cup sunflower seeds | 125 mL | ¼ cup oil (*C) | 60 mL |
| ½ cup sesame seeds | 125 mL | | |

Mix all of the ingredients together and blend in an electric blender in batches until smooth. Pour into ice cube trays and freeze until solid. Stir once or twice during freezing.

| Free of: M E W G | |
| --- | --- |
| Can be free of: C F | |
| Contains: S | |

# Ice Cream Cones

| 5 cups puffed rice | 1250 mL | ½ cup peanut | 125 mL |
| ⅓ cup milk-free margarine (*F, C) | 75 mL | butter (optional) | |
| | | ½ pound marsh-mallows (32 large) (*C) | 226 g |

Heat rice in shallow pan at 350°F (180°C) for 10 minutes. Pour into a large greased bowl. Melt margarine, peanut butter, and marshmallows in double boiler. Pour marshmallow mixture over puffed rice until mixture is coated. Pack mixture in bottom and sides of paper cups or greased custard cups, leaving centre hollow. Chill thoroughly. Fill with ice cream when needed.

# Vanilla Ice Cream

| | | | |
|---|---|---|---|
| 1 tablespoon unflavored gelatin | 15 mL | 2 tablespoons light corn syrup | 25 mL |
| 2 tablespoons cold water | 25 mL | 2½ tablespoons vegetable oil | 37 mL |
| ¼ cup granulated sugar | 60 mL | 2 teaspoons vanilla extract | 10 mL |
| 13 ounces soy formula concentrated liquid | 370 mL | | |

Soften gelatin in cold water in a saucepan. Add sugar and heat slowly to dissolve gelatin and sugar. Cool mixture. Add remaining ingredients. Blend in a blender until thick and creamy. Pour into ice cube tray or loaf pan or other container and place in freezer until icy. Return mixture to blender and blend until smooth. Return to freezer.

## Variations
Add fresh fruit or ½ cup (125 mL) chocolate syrup with remaining ingredients.

# Lime Sherbet

| | | | |
|---|---|---|---|
| ½ cup sugar | 125 mL | Pinch salt | |
| 3 cups water | 750 mL | 1 beaten egg white | |
| ¼ cup lime or lemon juice | 60 mL | | |

Combine sugar and water in a small saucepan and boil 5 minutes. Remove from heat and stir in juice and salt. Pour into refrigerator tray and let cool. Place in freezer and leave until outside edges are hard. Break up with spoon, add egg white and beat well. Return mixture to tray and freeze until firm.

## Apricot Sherbet

Free of: M E W G

Contains: C F S

Makes 1½ quarts or litres

| | | | |
|---|---|---|---|
| 1 envelope unflavored gelatin | | ¾ cup light corn syrup | 175 mL |
| ½ cup cold water | 125 mL | 3 tablespoons lemon juice | 40 mL |
| 3 cups (2 12-ounce cans) apricot nectar | 750 mL | ⅛ teaspoon salt | .5 mL |

Sprinkle gelatin on water in saucepan. Place over low heat, stirring constantly, until gelatin is dissolved. Stir in remaining ingredients. Pour into 2 refrigerator freezing trays and freeze until firm, about 1 hour. Break up in bowl and beat until light. Return to freezing trays and freeze until firm, 2–3 hours.

## Banana Pineapple Sherbet

Free of: M W G C

Contains: E S F

| | | | |
|---|---|---|---|
| 1½ cups crushed pineapple | 375 mL | ½ cup orange juice | 125 mL |
| ¾ cup confectioner's sugar | 175 mL | 6 tablespoons lemon juice | 90 mL |
| 1½ cups banana pulp (about 3 large bananas) | 375 mL | 2 egg whites | |

Combine pineapple and sugar; stir until dissolved. Add banana and juices. Place in refrigerator trays and freeze until nearly firm. Beat egg whites until stiff but not dry. Add fruit mixture gradually. Beat sherbet until light and fluffy. Return to trays and freeze until firm.

# *Orange Sherbet*

Makes 6–8 servings

| | | | |
|---|---|---|---|
| 1 can concentrated liquid soy milk | 384 mL | 1 6-ounce can frozen unsweetened orange juice concentrate, thawed | 170 g |
| 1 tablespoon lemon juice | 15 mL | ½ cup sugar | 125 mL |
| | | 1 teaspoon vanilla | 5 mL |

Remove lid from can of soy milk. Place opened can in freezer for 1½ hours or until crystals begin to form around edge of can. Pour into large chilled bowl and beat until slightly thick and foamy. Add lemon juice and continue beating until stiff peaks begin to form. Blend in thawed orange juice, sugar and vanilla. Pour into two refrigerator trays. Place in freezer for 1 hour, or until mixture becomes almost completely frozen. Spoon into bowl and beat until smooth and creamy. Pour into the refrigerator trays. Freeze for 1½ hours or until firm.

# GOURMET

Allergen-free cooking takes more time because everything has to be made from scratch so we have tried to choose recipes that are fairly simple. These gourmet recipes, however, are ones that require some extra thought and effort for special occasions. They are great for dinner parties and adventurous cooks.

| Free of: C S |
|---|
| Can be free of: M E W G F |

## Meat Tarts

Makes 18 tarts

18 slices of bread (as allowed) (*W, G)

1 cup bread cubes 250 mL or crumbs (use diet bread if needed) or ¾ cup oatmeal 175 mL

1 can mushroom soup or 1 can chicken and rice soup or 1 small can cream-style corn for gluten and wheat-free diets

1 teaspoon 5 mL Worcestershire sauce (*E)

½ pound ground 225 g beef

1 egg or egg replacer (*E)

Salt and pepper to taste

Onion

½ cup grated cheese 125 mL (omit for milk-free) (*M, F)

Make bread cups from slices of bread (or diet bread). Place in muffin tins. Mix all remaining ingredients, fill cups and bake at 350°F (180°C) for ½ hour. Can be reheated.

**Free of: E W G S**

**Can be free of: C F**

**Contains: M**

# *Cheese Minis*

Makes 50

| | | | |
|---|---|---|---|
| 1 cup rice flour | 250 mL | ¼ cup butter or margarine (*C, F) | 60 mL |
| 1 teaspoon sugar | 5 mL | 1 cup grated Cheddar cheese (*F) | 250 mL |
| ½ teaspoon salt | 2 mL | ½ cup milk | 125 mL |
| 2 teaspoons baking powder | 10 mL | | |

Sift flour, sugar, salt and baking powder together, then sift into mixing bowl. Add butter and blend with two knives. Add grated cheese and blend. Add milk. Stir with fork and roll out thinly onto floured board. Cut with knife into 1 inch squares (2.5 cm). Place on greased baking sheet. Bake at 375°F (190°C) for 15 minutes or until lightly browned.

**Free of: M E W G C S**

**Contains: F**

# *Shrimp in Aspic*

| | | | |
|---|---|---|---|
| 1 envelope unflavored gelatin | | ½ teaspoon salt | 2 mL |
| ⅓ cup cold water | 75 mL | 1 teaspoon curry powder | 5 mL |
| 2 tablespoons lemon juice | 30 mL | 1 small tin shrimp | |
| 1½ cups tomato juice | 375 mL | 1 cup chopped celery | 250 mL |

Soften gelatin in cold water. Bring juices to a boil and add softened gelatin, salt and curry powder. Stir until dissolved. Chill until slightly thickened. Add drained shrimp and celery. Serve on lettuce leaf and garnish with slivers of green pepper and sliced olives.

# Party Platter
# or Shishkabobs

| | | |
|---|---|---|
| Meat balls, cooked | Carrot sticks | Cherry tomatoes |
| Cocktail sausages | Cauliflower | Green pepper |
| Fish sticks | Celery | Shrimp |
| Vienna sausages | Cucumber | Cold meat, cut in cubes |
| Scallops | Pickles | Mandarin oranges |
| Onion Rings | Cheese cubes | Pineapple tidbits |
| Stuffed celery | Radishes | Grapes |

Choose foods which suit your diet to make up a party platter and let guests help themselves. Several different dips should be available. Many of these foods can be used to make shishkabobs. Give each guest a 6-inch (15 cm) wooden skewer to make his own favorite treat.

Free of: M

Can be free of: E W G C S

Contains: F

# Horseradish Dip

| | | | |
|---|---|---|---|
| 2 tablespoons horseradish | 30 mL | ½ cup chili sauce | 125 mL |
| 1 teaspoon meat sauce or ketchup (*S) | 5 mL | ⅓ cup mayonnaise (as allowed) (*E, W, G, C) | 75 mL |
| 2 teaspoons Worcestershire sauce | 10 mL | | |

Mix all ingredients well. Store in jar in refrigerator.

Free of: M W G

Can be free of: C F

Contains: E S

# Dill Dip

4 egg yolks

5 teaspoons prepared    25 mL
  mustard

1 teaspoon salt         5 mL

2 tablespoons dried     30 mL
  dill

½ teaspoon pepper       2 mL

1 tablespoon sugar      15 mL

1 cup oil (*C, F)       250 mL

2 tablespoons           30 mL
  vinegar

Beat egg yolks. Add next 5 ingredients and beat well. Add oil, one teaspoon at a time, beating constantly. Add vinegar and beat.

Free of: S

Can be free of: E W G C F

Contains: M

# Curry Dip

½ cup mayonnaise        125 mL
  (as allowed) (*E, W, G, C, F)

½ cup sour cream        125 mL

½ teaspoon lemon        2 mL
  juice

1 teaspoon curry        5 mL
  powder

Mix all ingredients well. Chill. Keep in refrigerator.

## Free of: M E W G
## Can be free of: C S
## Contains: F

# Chinese Beef

| | | | | |
|---|---|---|---|---|
| 2 pounds flank steak | 1 Kg | ¼ teaspoon ground ginger | 1 mL |
| 2 tomatoes | | ¼ cup soy sauce | 60 mL |
| 2 green peppers | | ½ teaspoon sugar (optional) (*S) | 2 mL |
| 2 tablespoons olive oil or other oil | 25 mL | 1 teaspoon cornstarch (*C) | 5 mL |
| 1 clove garlic, crushed | | ¼ cup water | 60 mL |
| 1 teaspoon salt | 5 mL | ¼ pound bean sprouts | 125 g |
| Dash of pepper | | | |

Cut steak in strips across the grain of the meat. Cut tomatoes in quarters; trim away seeds and ribs from green peppers and cut into big chunks. Heat oil in skillet. Add strips of beef, garlic, salt, pepper and ginger. Fry over high heat until brown on all sides. Season with soy sauce and sugar. Cover tightly and cook slowly for 5 minutes. Then toss in tomatoes, green peppers, and bring to boil; cover and cook briskly for 5 minutes. Make a paste of cornstarch and water. Add to beef mixture and cook until sauce thickens slightly. Add bean sprouts and stir occasionally until heated through. Serve with rice and green salad.

## Free of: M E W G
## Can be free of: C F S

# Potatoes in Shells

| | | | | |
|---|---|---|---|---|
| 6 medium baking potatoes | | 1 tablespoon sugar (optional) (*S) | 15 mL |
| 6 strips bacon | | 2 tablespoons vinegar | 25 mL |
| ¾ cup minced onion | 175 mL | ¼ cup minced green pepper | 60 mL |
| 1½ teaspoons salt | 7 mL | Milk-free margarine (*C, F) | |
| ¼ teaspoon pepper | 1 mL | | |
| ½ teaspoon celery seed | 2 mL | | |

Bake potatoes at 400°F (200°C) for about one hour. Cook bacon until crisp, drain and crumble. Sauté onion in bacon drippings. Add salt, pepper, celery seed, sugar, and vinegar. Heat mixture. Cut a thin piece from top of each potato and carefully scoop out inside. Do not break shells. Combine potato, vinegar mixture, crumbled bacon and green pepper. Stuff into shells and dot with margarine. Set in baking pan and broil slightly to heat mixture and lightly brown tops.

```
Free of: M E W G

Can be free of: C F

Contains: S
```

## Crêpes Suzanna

Makes a soft, tender pancake that can be rolled. Serves 4–6.

| | | | |
|---|---|---|---|
| ¾ cup uncooked rice | 175 mL | 1½ teaspoons oil (*C, F) | 7 mL |
| ½ cup dried yellow split peas | 125 mL | Juice of 1 lemon | |
| 3 cups water, divided | 750 mL | 1 teaspoon salt | 5 mL |
| | | Confectioner's sugar | |
| | | Lemon slices, strips of peel | |

In separate bowls soak rice and peas in 1½ cups (375 mL) water for 8 hours or overnight. Drain each, reserving liquids separately. In blender or food processor purée peas and ½ cup (125 mL) reserved liquid (or water if necessary) until smooth; pour into bowl. Purée rice and 1¼ cup (300 mL) reserved liquid (or water if necessary) until smooth; stir into pea mixture. Add oil, 2 teaspoons (10 mL) lemon juice and salt. Into a large, well-greased skillet over medium-high heat pour scant ¼ cup (50 mL) batter for each crêpe and cook over medium heat until tops look dry and bottoms are lightly browned. Turn and cook 1–2 minutes longer. Sprinkle with some remaining juice and sugar. Garnish with additional sugar, lemon slice and strips of peel.

Free of: M E W

Can be free of: C F

Contains: G S

# Cantonese Duck

Serves 4

| | | | | |
|---|---|---|---|---|
| 2 | 2–2½ pound wild ducks | 1–1.25 Kg | 2 tablespoons soy sauce (*F) | 25 mL |
| | Garlic salt | | 1 cup apricot preserves | 250 mL |
| | Pepper | | | |
| | Sprigs parsley | | 1 tablespoon lemon juice | 15 mL |
| 1 | lemon, halved | | | |
| 6 | slices bacon | | 1 teaspoon grated orange peel (*F) | 5 mL |
| ½ | cup beer | 125 mL | ¼ cup oil (*C, F) | 60 mL |
| ¼ | cup dry mustard | 60 mL | | |
| ½ | teaspoon salt | 2 mL | | |

Sprinkle ducks inside and out with garlic salt and pepper. Place 2 sprigs parsley and ½ lemon in cavity of each. Cover breasts with bacon and fasten with string. To make Cantonese sauce, stir beer into dry mustard. Add remaining ingredients except oil and heat in double boiler over hot water. Place duck, breasts up, in baking pan. Roast in preheated 350°F (180°C) oven for 15 minutes per pound (.5 Kg), basting frequently with oil and once with Cantonese sauce. Carve ducks. Serve with white rice and remaining Cantonese sauce.

Free of: M C

Can be free of: W G F

Contains: E S

# Baba au Rum

| | | | |
|---|---|---|---|
| 8 | large eggs | 8 tablespoons fine breadcrumbs (suitable to diet) (*W, G) | 120 mL |
| 8 | tablespoons sugar | 120 mL | |

Separate eggs, beat egg whites until very stiff. Sift dry crumbs. Cream egg yolks and sugar until light and thick. Fold creamed mixture into egg whites. Sprinkle breadcrumbs on batter and fold well. Pour into an ungreased 9-inch (23 cm) tube pan and bake at 375°F (190°C) for ¾ hour.

## Syrup

| | | | |
|---|---|---|---|
| 1 cup water | 250 mL | Slices of lemon and/or | |
| ½ cup sugar | 125 mL | oranges (*F) | |
| ½ cup honey | 125 mL | 4 tablespoons rum | 60 mL |

Mix together water, sugar, honey and fruit. Cook 20 minutes. Remove lemon and orange slices, cool, then add rum. Saturate the cake with syrup as soon as it has baked. Chill. Cake will fall slightly and will keep over one week if kept chilled. Serve with whipping cream or substitute.

ree of: M E W G C S

ontains: F

# Warm Banana Royale

Makes 4–6 servings

| | | | |
|---|---|---|---|
| 5 bananas | | ¼ cup honey | 60 mL |
| 1 apple, diced | | ⅓ cup coconut | 75 mL |
| ⅓ cup orange juice | 75 mL | | |
| 2 tablespoons lemon juice | 25 mL | | |

Toast coconut in 200°F (90°C) oven until brown. Cut bananas into half-inch (1.25 cm) slices and place in a small shallow baking dish with the apple. Blend juices with honey and pour over fruit. Bake at 400°F (200°C) for 10 minutes or until bananas are warm. Sprinkle with toasted coconut.

Free of: E C

Can be free of: M W G F

Contains: S

# Café-au-Lait Dessert

Makes 6 servings

1 envelope unflavored gelatin
¼ cup cold water — 60 mL
2 cups boiling water — 500 mL
2 teaspoons instant coffee (*W, G) — 10 mL

¼ cup sugar — 60 mL
2 tablespoons instant chocolate or cocoa (*M, W, F) — 25 mL
¾ cup dry skim-milk powder (*M) — 175 mL

Soften gelatin in cold water. Add boiling water, coffee, sugar and chocolate and stir until dissolved. Chill in refrigerator until syrupy, at least 40 minutes. Beat mixture and slowly add dry milk powder. Pour into dishes and chill until set.

**Note:** Substitute milk-free whipped topping for milk powder and fold into gelatin mixture.

Free of: E W G

Can be free of: M C F S

# Crinkle Cups

6 squares semi-sweet or unsweetened chocolate (*M, S)

2 tablespoons milk-free margarine (*M, C, F) — 30 mL

Heat chocolate and margarine over hot water until chocolate is partly melted. Remove from hot water; stir rapidly until ingredients are well blended and mixture is thick. Using a teaspoon, cover inside surface of 10 large paper baking cups with thin layer of mixture. Set in muffin pans; chill until hard. About 10 minutes before serving, fill with ice cream or pudding. Chill in refrigerator before peeling off paper.

# CANDIES AND SNACKS

Most candies and snacks are loaded with empty calories. This section contains more nutritious ingredients than store-bought snack food. Most of these recipes use honey, molasses, sesame seeds, or fruit instead of chemical flavorings and preservatives.

If your family likes a treat (and whose doesn't) try these. A snack should be as carefully nutritious as the meals you serve.

Free of: M E W G

Can be free of: F

Contains: C S

## O Henrys

| | | | |
|---|---|---|---|
| 1 cup sugar | 250 mL | 1 cup peanut | 250 mL |
| 1 cup corn | 250 mL | butter (*F) | |
| syrup (*F) | | 6 cups cereal | 1500 mL |
| | | (cornflakes, rice flakes) | |

Heat sugar, corn syrup and peanut butter until melted and hot but *not* boiling. Mix with 6 cups of cereal. Roll into logs and place on waxed paper. Allow to harden. May be frosted with butterscotch chips, chocolate chips, carob chips or butter icing. Rather than making logs, batter can be spread into a greased 13 inch × 9 inch (33 × 23 cm) pan.

Free of: E

Can be free of: M C F W G S

## Garlic Buttered Popcorn or Puffed Cereal

Add sliced garlic clove to butter or milk-free margarine (*M, C, F). Cook until garlic flavor is adequate. Add to freshly popped corn or puffed cereal (*W, G, S). Heat 5 minutes at 350°F (180°C).

Free of: M E W G

Can be free of: F

Contains: C S

# Popcorn Balls

| | | | |
|---|---|---|---|
| 5 quarts popped corn | 5.5 L | ½ cup light corn syrup (*F) | 125 mL |
| 2 cups sugar | 500 mL | 1 teaspoon vinegar | 5 mL |
| 1½ cups water | 375 mL | 1 teaspoon vanilla | 5 mL |
| ½ teaspoon salt | 2 mL | Colored sugar (optional) | |

Keep popcorn hot and crisp in oven at 300°F (150°C). Grease sides of saucepan and combine in it sugar, water, salt, corn syrup and vinegar. Cook to hard-ball stage. Add vanilla. Pour slowly over hot popped corn, mixing well to coat every kernel. Press into balls with greased hands. May be coated with colored sugar.

Free of: M E W G

Can be free of: C F

Contains: S

# Cream Fudge

| | | | |
|---|---|---|---|
| 2 cups brown sugar | 500 mL | 2 tablespoons oil (*C, F) | 30 mL |
| 6 tablespoons water | 90 mL | ½ teaspoon vanilla | 2 mL |

Mix sugar, water and oil. Stir constantly until boiling point is reached. Allow to boil to soft-ball stage (2 minutes). Add vanilla. Beat firmly (immersing pot in cold water helps) until candy turns lighter in color. Pour into greased pan and cut into squares.

# Goat's Milk Carob Fudge

Free of: E W G S

Can be free of: M C F

### Makes 1 dozen squares

| | | | | |
|---|---|---|---|---|
| 1½ cups honey | 375 mL | ⅓ cup carob powder | 75 mL |
| ⅔ cup goat's milk | 150 mL | ⅓ cup chopped nuts | 75 mL |
| 2 tablespoons butter | 30 mL | 1 teaspoon vanilla | 5 mL |
| or milk-free margarine | | | |
| (*M, C, F) | | | |

Place honey, milk, butter and carob powder in a heavy saucepan. Heat, stirring constantly, until mixture is well blended and then cook without stirring until thermometer registers 238°F (114°C). Cool to lukewarm and then beat until mixture loses its shininess. Work in the vanilla and nuts. Pour into a greased pan. Cool and cut into squares.

Can be free of: M G C F

Contains: E W S

# Sesame Crisps

| | | | |
|---|---|---|---|
| ¼ cup butter or | 60 mL | ½ cup wheat | 125 mL |
| milk-free margarine | | starch (*G) | |
| (*M, C, F) | | ½ teaspoon baking | 2 mL |
| ½ cup brown sugar | 125 mL | powder (*C) | |
| (firmly packed) | | ½ cup sesame seeds | 125 mL |
| 1 beaten egg | | | |
| ½ teaspoon vanilla | 2 mL | | |

Cream butter and sugar. Add egg and vanilla. Sift wheat starch and baking powder and beat until smooth. Add sesame seeds and blend well. Drop by small teaspoons onto a well-greased cookie sheet. Leave a 2-inch (5 cm) space between each one as they will spread. Bake at 375°F (190°C) for 10 minutes. Remove from cookie sheet immediately.

| Free of: M E W G C |
|---|
| Can be free of: S F |

# Non-Drip Popsicles

Dissolve one package unflavored gelatin in one cup boiling water. Add 1½ cups permitted juice (F*). Sweeten to taste with sugar or honey (*S). Pour into molds and freeze. Serve as popsicles.

| Free of: M E W G C F |
|---|
| Contains: S |

# Puffed Rice Brittle

| 1 cup sugar | 250 mL | 2 cups puffed rice | 500 mL |
|---|---|---|---|
| Pinch of salt | | ½ teaspoon vanilla | 2 mL |

Put sugar in heavy iron frying pan to melt. Stir until melted and light brown in color. Add salt, puffed rice and vanilla. Mix together and pour at once on a greased slab or dish. With wet rolling pin, roll out flat and when cold, break into pieces.

| Free of: E W G S |
|---|
| Can be free of: M C F |

# Sesame Honey Candy

| ¼ cup butter or milk- | 60 mL | 1 cup grated coconut | 250 mL |
|---|---|---|---|
| free margarine (*M, C, F) | | ½ teaspoon vanilla | 2 mL |
| ½ cup sesame seeds | 125 mL | ¼ cup honey | 60 mL |

In a large frying pan melt butter on low heat. Add sesame seeds and coconut. Stir for 5 minutes. Remove pan from heat and add vanilla and honey. Mix well. Place candy in refrigerator for 1 hour or in freezer for ½ hour, until mixture can be rolled into little balls. Keep refrigerated.

# BEVERAGES

Beverages can be quite restricted when certain foods are eliminated. For those who have to drink soy milk, read on for ideas on how to disguise it. There are also great ideas for homemade shakes, non-caffeine tea, and breakfast drinks.

Free of: E W G

Can be free of: M S F

Contains: C

## *Liquado*

| | | | |
|---|---|---|---|
| 1 cup milk or | 250 mL | 1 teaspoon vanilla | 5 mL |
| soy milk (*M) | | 1 tablespoon honey | 15 mL |
| 1 banana | | or sweetener (*S) | |

Place all ingredients in blender and liquefy—makes a delicious milk-shake drink.

### *Variations*
If allowed,

| | |
|---|---|
| Add 1 tablespoon peanut butter (*F) | 15 mL |
| Add 2 tablespoon protein powder | 25 mL |
| Add ½ cup fresh strawberries (*F) | 125 mL |
| Add 1 tablespoon sesame seed butter | 15 mL |

## *Nut Milk*

| | | | |
|---|---|---|---|
| ¼ cup of any | 60 mL | 8 ounces water | 250 mL |
| tolerated seed or nut | | | |

Place all ingredients in a blender and whiz until desired consistency is reached.

| Free of: M E W G C S F | *Coconut Milk or Cream* |
|---|---|

| 1 16-ounce package shredded coconut | 450 g | 2½ cups boiling water | 625 mL |
|---|---|---|---|

Add water to coconut in medium-sized bowl. Let stand for ½ hour. Place in blender (optional), then into a bottle and refrigerate. After milk has separated, the cream may be whipped.

| Free of: E W G C<br><br>Can be free of: M S F | *Hot or Cold Carob Milk* |
|---|---|

| 3 tablespoons carob powder | 40 mL | 4 cups milk or soy milk (*M) | 1 L |
|---|---|---|---|
| 1 tablespoon powdered goat's skim milk or dry soy milk (*M) | 15 mL | ½ teaspoon smooth peanut butter (*F) | 2 mL |
| 1–2 tablespoons brown sugar, honey or molasses (*S) | 15–25 mL | ½ ripe banana | |

Combine dry ingredients with 1 cup (250 mL) of milk. Mix well, add remaining milk, peanut butter and banana. Serve hot or cold. For egg nog add 1 well-beaten egg.

When preparing carob drinks, best results are obtained with a blender; or use a hand beater to whip the dry ingredients into the liquid thoroughly.

Free of: M E W G C S

Can be free of: F

# Nut and Seed Milk

| | | | |
|---|---|---|---|
| ¼ cup sunflower seed kernels | 60 mL | 2 tablespoons honey Sea salt to taste | 25 mL |
| ¾ cup cashews or blanched almonds (*F) | 125 mL | ½ teaspoon soy milk powder | 2 mL |
| 3 cups cold water | 750 mL | | |

Place seeds and nuts and one cup (250 mL) water into the blender and let soak 15 minutes. Blend until smooth. Add remaining ingredients and blend. Serve very cold. Try adding a little peanut butter and a banana for variety.

Free of: M E W G C

Can be free of: S F

# Fruit Shake

*Base*

| | | | |
|---|---|---|---|
| ¼ cup soy bean milk | 60 mL | 1 tablespoon sugar (optional) (*S) | 15 mL |
| ¼ cup cold water | 60 mL | ½ cup fruit juice (orange juice (*F), sweetened stewed apricots (*F), or pineapple juice) | 125 mL |
| ½ cup crushed ice | 125 mL | | |
| 1 tablespoon lemon juice | 15 mL | | |

Combine all ingredients in container with tight-fitting lid. Cover and shake well, or whiz in a blender. Serve at once.

# Sesame Seed Milk

| 2 cups water | 500 mL | ¼ cup sesame seeds | 50 mL |

Whiz water and sesame seeds in blender for 2 minutes. Strain if desired. Drink can be flavored with molasses, banana, carob powder, honey, fruit concentrate, dates or raisins.

This drink can also be prepared with 2 cups (500 mL) water and 4 tablespoons (50 mL) tahini. (Tahini is a sesame paste available in health food stores.)

# Flavorings for Soy Bean Milk

To improve the flavor of soy milk, one or more of the following may be added to one cup:

| 1 teaspoon lime juice | 5 mL |
| 1 tablespoon molasses | 15 mL |
| 1 tablespoon honey | 15 mL |
| ¾ cup frozen raspberries | 175 mL |
| 2 tablespoons fruit syrup | 25 mL |
| 2 tablespoons maple syrup | 25 mL |
| 2 tablespoons malt syrup | 25 mL |
| 1 pinch salt | |
| 2 teaspoons vanilla | 10 mL |
| 1 banana (in blender) | |
| Chocolate syrup to taste | |

# Quick Coolers

These beverages are best when made in a blender; however, most can be made with a beater. The liquid in each recipe can be milk or soy milk.

## Vanilla Shake

| | |
|---|---|
| 1 cup liquid | 250 mL |
| ½ teaspoon vanilla | 2 mL |
| ½ cup water | 125 mL |
| Sugar, if needed | |

## Chocolate Shake

| | |
|---|---|
| ½ cup liquid, diluted if necessary | 125 mL |
| 1 tablespoon instant chocolate | 15 mL |

## Mocha Drink

| | |
|---|---|
| ½ cup liquid | 125 mL |
| ½ cup coffee | 125 mL |

## Apricot Drink

| | |
|---|---|
| ½ cup liquid | 125 mL |
| ½ cup apricot nectar | 125 mL |

## Hawaiian Drink

| | |
|---|---|
| ½ cup liquid | 125 mL |
| 1 teaspoon sugar | 5 mL |
| ½ cup pineapple juice | 125 mL |

## Banana Drink

| | |
|---|---|
| 1 cup liquid | 250 mL |
| 1 tablespoon honey | 15 mL |
| 1 banana | |
| Crushed ice | |

A blender is essential here.

# Index

‡ definitely free of
★ could/can be free of